Morsel & Martha's

ADVENTURES in

COOKING

by

Mary J. Pelzel

MORSEL & MARTHA'S *ADVENTURES in* **COOKING**

First Edition

Copyright 2002 Mary J. Pelzel
All Rights Reserved
No part of this book may be reproduced in any form or by any electronic or mechanical means, including information storage or retrieval systems, without written permission from the publisher.

Published By   Mary J. Pelzel
P.O. Box 490
Selah, WA 98942

ISBN 0-9724316-0-8

Morsel & Martha's *Adventures* in **COOKING**

TABLE OF CONTENTS

INTRODUCTION	IV
SPECIAL DEDICATION	V
DEDICATION	VI
ACKNOWLEDGMENTS	VII
RECIPE LEGEND & QUALITY CHECK INSTRUCTIONS	VIII
APPETIZERS (MORSELS)	1
BREADS—QUICK & NOT SO QUICK (YEAST)	9
BREAKFAST & "EGGIE" STUFF	21
DESSERTS	33
MEATS	47
PASTA	59
POULTRY	67
RICE	75
SALADS	81
SANDWICHES	89
SEAFOOD	97
SOUPS, STEWS & CHILI	105
VEGETABLES	113
INDEX	124-132

INTRODUCTION

My inspiration for this cookbook was a dinner request by my husband for a pasta dish that we had previously enjoyed. This request was not easily granted because I am constantly trying new recipes and rarely prepare the same dish twice. My recipe collection is extensive and not very organized. So, as I'm searching and digging through recipe cards, newspaper clippings, magazines, and books trying to find a recipe that sounds like his request, I decided it was time to organize.

The cookbook MORSEL & MARTHA'S *ADVENTURES in* **COOKING** is the result. When I had my catering and baking enterprise, a business consultant instructed me to NEVER give out any of my recipes. What fun are recipes if you can't share them?

As you will see, I cook for fun not necessarily because I know what I'm doing. I'm not a dietitian, can't supply exact exchanges for special diets, or daily values of vitamins and minerals. The entries in my book were chosen for their interesting appearance, great tastes, and "fun" aspects. Cooking is fun if you make it that way. Remember entering the kitchen doesn't necessitate donning a hard hat and battle fatigues. Lots of family, lots of friends, and lots of food create lots of fun and lots of memories.

As Morsel and Martha guide you through the book, you will notice that each recipe has stars by the title. These stars designate degree of difficulty. One star being the easiest and five stars the most involved. None of the recipes are hard, but some may require a little more effort than others. They are worth it!

You will find that I'm big on fresh herbs--just love em!!! I grow them not only for their use in the kitchen, but for their ornamentation in the garden and the home. They attract the birds and butterflies as well as my kitchen shears. The use for fresh herbs ranges from the bud vase to the meatloaf. Try growing some of your own. Most are hardy, easy to grow and don't require a lot of space. Plant thyme (lemon would be nice) in between pathway stones. It smells so good when walked on and crushed. Have some mint, rosemary or sage by the door so you can rub it in your hands when you walk by to release the fragrant oils. Once you have fresh parsley, chives, and cilantro within easy reach, you will never want dried again.

There will be a wine recommendation only if I have discovered one that melds specifically with a certain dish. Otherwise, I would suggest lining up 3 or 4 bottles that might work and try them all. Even if you don't care for the recipe, you are guaranteed an enjoyable experience in dining and sampling a touch of the grape.

Now you are ready to turn the page, invite some friends over, and cook up some fun!

A SPECIAL DEDICATION

Who is Morsel? Why choose a mouse as a mascot for a cookbook? Well I have two reasons.

The first is my dad Glenn L. Peterson, a retired building contractor with a shop in Wapato. He now focuses his attentions on crafting specialty items such as grandfather clocks and his garden where he grows wonderful blueberries and herbs. Over the years, Dad has helped me with many projects. The plans for these projects have been drawn in his shop. Some of the shop's interior décor has been documented on these plans. When you enter through the side door, you will see cobwebs (with the occasional spider) artfully draped to frame the windows. The sawdust on the floor and the smell of varnish and stains add to the ambiance. More elusive but ever present are the "pet" mice. Every drawing that Dad has done for me depicts these busy little creatures. On a fireplace project you would see a tiny mouse scurrying across the top of the mantle. A kitchen project had a mouse running along the counter top and another peeking in through the window. You get the idea. As the little mice were transferred from shop space to Dad's drawing board, so have they been transferred to my cookbook.

Secondly, I would like to remember my good friend, Betty Wilcox. She passed away in November, 2001. She was an avid collector of mice in all shapes and forms. She had rooms full of the creatures. There were stuffed mice, ceramic mice, refrigerator magnet mice, and decorative mice for the holidays. When you received a birthday card from her, there was always a mouse on it. Even "Mom Betty's" car could be recognized by the mouse that adhered to her car window. We will always have a place in our hearts for her.

So in this small way, I am honoring and remembering Dad and Mom Betty. This is why a little gray mouse has been transformed into a charming and endearing character named Morsel.

On the lighter side, Morsel's friend Martha was created so that Morsel would not be lonely. Martha is a happy little pig that just loves hamburgers. Her Dagwood-style hamburgers are absolutely amazing. One would think you could never get your mouth around one of those things, but somehow she manages. These bites are true mouthfuls.

So Morsel and his friend Martha have evolved into MORSEL & MARTHA'S ADVENTURES in COOKING. I need to note at this time that it is only coincidental that Martha is also my mother's name!

Bon Appetit!

DEDICATION

I want to dedicate this book with love to my children Ron and Danielle, who think Mom's a good cook and to my wonderful husband David, for being such a willing guinea pig for so many years.

ACKNOWLEDGMENTS

My book and the characters of Morsel and Martha have come to life at "The Hideaway," our mountain home where we entertain family and friends on a regular basis. This project has been kept under wraps from beginning to end. Everyone that I worked with was sworn to secrecy. Afraid of the unknown, I thought I might change my mind and didn't want anyone to know of this unborn child until I actually gave birth. The delivery date was set for October 1, 2002. The date of conception was February 1, 2002.

I want to thank my husband David for his encouragement, patience, and willingness to try new creations from the kitchen. We would diet like crazy during the work week and eat like crazy during the weekend. Friday night the apron went on and it didn't come off until Sunday night. I was "in the lab." Most of my experiments were successful, but every once in awhile we went looking for the Mr. Yuk stickers!

My good friend Floyd A. Broadbent was my first official contact as a publisher to be. He saw potential in my project. His enthusiasm and encouragement really helped me to proceed. I will forever keep his chicken sketch.

The next contact was to the copyright attorney. I had to be legal you know. Michelle Bos was wonderful and very encouraging. She gave me so much help and information. If nothing else, I have learned not to be afraid to ask questions.

Mark Fischer of Lightning Press was the only printer for me. I felt comfortable and in capable hands. His patient and friendly ways of helping me through the whole printing process has made a hard job easier.

I am deeply grateful to my proofreader Kathy Otto for the generous time she has given to me and my book. If it wasn't for her expertise, "MORSEL & MARTHA'S *ADVENTURES in* **COOKING**" would be one long run-on sentence. I now know the difference between a dash and a hyphen. Thank you, Kathy.

My son Ron, who has referred to me over the years as "Betty Crocker," has been helping me with computer questions over the last few months and probably wondering what Mom is up to now. I don't relate to computers other than to locate the keyboard and type. As a computer guru, he has been most helpful. Thanks Ronnie!

Finally, my daughter Danielle was the person who unknowingly helped to make the final decision to go ahead with the "Morsel" project. Every time she would call and say "Mom, I'm having one of my papers published," I would think if she can do it, so can I!

Martha's Recipe Difficulty Legend:

- * EASY
-
- * * FAST
-
- * * * ALLOW MORE TIME
-
- * * * * A LITTLE MORE EFFORT REQUIRED
-
- * * * * * HARDER, BUT WORTH THE EFFORT!

Morsel's Quality Check Instructions:

There are several recipes in MORSEL & MARTHA'S *ADVENTURES* that have alcohol as an ingredient. I love to cook with wine, but quality assurance of the wine is a must. When assembling ingredients for such recipes, always remember to set out a glass for the cook. Directly after popping the cork on a bottle of wine, dispense some into the previously set aside glass. After proper sampling to verify that quality and taste are what is required for the dish you are preparing, then feel free to continue with the recipe. If the first bottle does not meet with the cook's standards, then open another, and so on . . .

Note: Sometimes quality assurance takes more than one glass.

Legend & Quality Check

** PASTRAMI BITES

While our daughter was studying in Germany, she was served this tasty morsel when she was a dinner guest of Maj. David Hilber. She loved it and brought the recipe home. These are melt in your mouth good!

Ingredients:

2 8-ounce packages refrigerator crescent rolls
1/2 pound deli pastrami, sliced paper thin
1/2 cup soft cream cheese with chives and onions
1/3 cup Dijon-style mustard
Fresh chives, chopped to sprinkle on top

Directions:

Preheat oven to 375 degrees. Separate crescent rolls into triangles. Cut triangles in half lengthwise to make 2 smaller triangles. Cut pastrami into 1 x 2 inch strips. Spread 1 teaspoon cream cheese and 1/2 teaspoon mustard on each triangle, leaving about 1/4 inch of the pointed end uncovered. Stack 3 pieces of pastrami at wide end of triangle. Beginning at wide end, roll up triangle and place on an ungreased cookie sheet with point side down. Sprinkle with fresh chives. Bake 12-16 minutes or until golden brown. Serve warm. Yields 32 rolls.

* BISCUIT BUNDLES

I think appetizers should be easy to prepare. This one is easy and very yummy. The cream cheese, green onion and garlic whet the appetite for just one more bite...

Ingredients:

1 package 16.3 ounce refrigerator biscuits (I used Pillsbury Grands)
2-3 green onions, sliced
1 small package cream cheese
Garlic Salt
Butter, optional

Directions:

Separate biscuits and cut into quarters. Pat out each piece and put a 1/2 inch cube of cream cheese in center. Press 2-4 pieces of onion into cheese. Pinch edges of dough together to make small round bundles. Sprinkle lightly with garlic salt and bake on ungreased baking sheet 10-15 minutes or until golden brown. The bundles will open slightly during cooking. Dot with butter if desired. Remove from baking sheet. Serve warm. Yields 32 bundles.

Morsels

* * DATE-GARLIC-BACON BITES

This combo sounds bizarre! Believe me your guests will be hovering around the oven waiting for the next pan to come out. You will need more than one pan. What's so nice about these is that they can be made way in advance and frozen.

Ingredients:

1 pound package of bacon (I prefer peppered bacon)
Garlic--approximately 20 cloves
1 package of pitted dates

Directions:

Slice the bacon strips into thirds so that you have pieces 3-4 inches long. Insert a clove of garlic into the opening of the date. If the cloves are large, cut them to fit. Wrap each stuffed date with a strip of bacon, secure with toothpicks. (Can be frozen at this point.) Place on ungreased baking sheet that has a rim around it and bake at 350 for 20 minutes or so. The bacon should be well browned and the garlic soft. The frozen ones don't have to be thawed. They just require more cooking time. Yields about 30 pieces.

* MUSHROOM SPREAD

If you're a mushroom lover, this ones for you. Stirs up in minutes and is oh-so-good. Mushrooms, Parmesan cheese, and a little "zing" from Italian dressing are delectable when served with small rye bread slices or crackers.

Ingredients:

2 cups mayonnaise
8 ounces of cheddar cheese, shredded
2 8-ounce cans of mushrooms stems and pieces, drained
2/3 cup of grated Parmesan cheese
1 package of dry Italian dressing mix
Paprika for garnish
Fresh chives, chopped for garnish

Directions:

Mix all ingredients together but the paprika and chives. Spoon into a 1 1/2 quart baking dish. Sprinkle with paprika and chives. Bake at 350 degrees for 35 minutes uncovered. Serve with rye bread or crackers. Yields about 4 cups.

Morsels

* PECANS--ORANGE AND SPICY

You can eat these perky pecans by the handfuls. Brown sugar, orange juice, and chili make these nuts a sensational starter.

Ingredients:
2 tablespoons of brown sugar
2 tablespoons orange juice concentrate
1 1/2 tablespoons butter or margarine
1/2 teaspoon salt
1/2 teaspoon chili powder (This amount gives flavor, but doesn't cover up the nutty taste.)
1/2 teaspoon freshly ground black or cayenne pepper (or use both!)
1 1/2 cups coarsely chopped pecans

Directions:
In a skillet combine sugar, orange juice, butter, salt, chili powder, and pepper. Cook over medium heat until sugar dissolves. Remove from heat and stir in pecans. Spread on lightly greased baking sheet. Bake at 350 degrees for 6 minutes or until toasted. Stir frequently during baking time. They will burn easily. Cool before eating. Yields about 1 1/2 cups.

* * CAJUN POWER WINGS

You have to line up the napkins for this one. Hot pepper sauce and balsamic vinegar blend to give the wings a splendidly robust flavor that will have you licking the sauce off your fingers so that you don't miss any.

Ingredients:
4 pounds chicken wings (tips removed)
2 teaspoons balsamic vinegar
2 teaspoons olive oil
4 tablespoons hot pepper sauce (I use Cajun Power Spicy Garlic Pepper Sauce.)
Salt and freshly ground black pepper

Directions:
Place chicken in large bowl. In a separate bowl combine vinegar, oil, pepper sauce, salt and pepper to taste. Pour sauce over chicken and toss to coat every piece. Transfer chicken to large baking sheet that has been coated with cooking spray. Roast at 500 degrees on top oven rack for 30 minutes. Turn wings and roast another 20-30 minutes. Wings are done when well browned and crisp. Serves 4.

* CHILI PASTRY OLE'

Don't turn your back on this after it comes out of the oven or you won't get any! These are full of green chilies and dripping with melted cheese, salsa, and sour cream. What could be better?

Ingredients:
1 package of refrigerated pie crust--2 sheets
1 can (4 ounces) chopped green chilies, drained
1 cup of shredded cheddar cheese (sharp or medium)
1 cup of Monterey Jack cheese, shredded
1/2 teaspoon chili powder
Salsa and sour cream
Green onions, sliced for garnish

Directions:
On an ungreased baking sheet, place one sheet of pie pastry. Sprinkle chilies and cheeses over pastry to within 1/2 inch of edge. Sprinkle with chili powder. Top with second pastry, seal edges, and prick top with a fork. Sprinkle a little more chili powder on top. Bake at 450 degrees for 10-15 minutes or until golden brown. Cool for 10 minutes and cut into wedges. Serve with salsa, sour cream, and onions. OLE'!!!
Serves 6.

* * SAUSAGE & BACON ROLL-UPS

These are a little bit of magic. Everywhere I take them, they disappear! So get out your wand and make some.

Ingredients:
1/4 cup butter or margarine
1/2 cup water
1 1/2 cups herb-seasoned stuffing mix
1/4 pound bulk pork sausage
1 large egg, lightly beaten
12 slices bacon, cut in half
1 tablespoon fresh chives, chopped
1 tablespoon fresh parsley, finely chopped

Directions:
Melt butter in saucepan. Add water and bring to a boil. Remove from heat. Stir in stuffing mix, chives, and parsley. Mix in sausage and egg. Cover and chill 30 minutes. Shape into 24 tiny "logs." Wrap a piece of bacon around each log and secure with toothpick. Place on rack of broiler pan. Bake at 375 degrees for 20 minutes. Turn logs and bake another 20 minutes or until browned. Drain on paper towels and cool.
Yields 2 dozen.

Morsels

* CELERY WITH GORGONZOLA

Next to opening a can of nuts or tearing open a bag of potato chips, this is the easiest appetizer I know of. The flavor blend of crisp, juicy celery and rich, tangy Gorgonzola is incredibly good. Serve them with cocktails or just as a snack.

Ingredients:

12 crisp stalks celery, leaves left on
1/2 cup Gorgonzola cheese
1/2 cup cream cheese
Fresh chives

Directions:

Wash and dry the celery stalks, trim the root ends. The long filled stalks with the leaves on the ends are impressive on a plate. Sometimes it's nicer to have the celery cut into 2-3 inch pieces for easier nibbling. When preparing your celery, take an extra minute to destring it. Those outer strings can be tough to bite through and all too chewy. In a small bowl, mash the cheeses together until smooth. Fill the celery with the cheese mixture. Smooth the filling and sprinkle with chopped chives. Chill before serving. Serves 6.

* DIVINE DILL DIP

The savory, down to earth flavor of dill brings a touch of the extraordinary to this dip. Serve it with fresh vegetables or as a topper for baked potatoes.

Ingredients:

1 cup sour cream
1 cup mayonnaise
1 heaping tablespoon fresh dill weed
1 teaspoon Beau Monde
Small green onion sliced
Fresh parsley, finely chopped for garnish

Directions:

Plan ahead. The flavor is best when dip has been refrigerated for several hours. Mix all ingredients except parsley in bowl. Garnish with fresh parsley. Yields about 2 cups.

SPECIAL IDEAS FOR SPECIAL TIMES

"Special" pottery: Many veggies and fruits can be hollowed out and used for pottery. Bell peppers (green, red, yellow, or orange) can be used as dip dishes. Be sure to choose peppers with stems intact. Cut top off of pepper and clean out seeds. Fill pepper with dip or salsa. Replace top on pepper. Serve peppers surrounded by chips or fresh veggies. A zucchini hollowed out can make a beautiful and unique substitution for an olive tray. Slice a small zucchini in half lengthwise. Scoop out seeds. Fill hollowed out space with black and green olives. Drizzle with olive oil and sprinkle with snipped fresh herbs such as parsley, chives, thyme, or oregano. Cut the top off of a squash, remove seeds and bake until tender and fill with soup. Try using round bread loaves with tops cut off and inside portions removed as serving bowls for chili or dip.

Nothing says special like flowers. There are many edible flowers such as nasturtiums, violets, rose petals, and lavender that can be added to salads and desserts that add that touch of special. Dianthus, pansies, and daylillies are especially nice for desserts. At Thanksgiving, take a small pumpkin, hollow it out, and fill it with flowers for an extraordinary center piece.

ROMANCING THE HOME. Don't forget this. Light some candles, turn on some music, and put a few flowers in a vase. These could range from large and purple country clovers to long stemmed red roses. Any little touch of something blooming will work.

Special

BREADS

Quick & Not So Quick - Yeast

* * BLACK PEPPER AND ONION BREAD

This is one of my favorite recipes for the bread machine. The aroma is out of this world. There's just enough black pepper to set off the flavor of the onions. This bread is excellent for salad croutons, bread crumbs or turkey dressing.

Ingredients:
1 1/4 cups water
3 1/4 cups white bread flour *
2 tablespoons dry milk
2 tablespoons brown sugar
1 1/2 teaspoons salt
2 tablespoons butter
1/2 cup dried onions
1/3-1/2 teaspoon onion powder
1 teaspoon black pepper
3 teaspoons active dry yeast

Directions:
Place all ingredients in your bread machine and push start. This makes a large loaf.

*Note--You can use all-purpose flour, but it doesn't have enough protein to produce the quality of bread that bread flour will.

* * CHERRY CHOCOLATE BREAD

This moist, rich chocolaty bread is wonderful--almost a dessert. I like to fix it as a special treat for a Valentine's Day brunch.

Ingredients:
1 1/4 cups water
2 cups white bread flour
1 cup wheat bread flour
2 tablespoons dry milk
1/4 cup molasses
1 1/2 teaspoons salt
1/2 cup chocolate chips
1/2 cup dried cherries
1 tablespoon Triple Sec liqueur
1/2-1 teaspoon fresh orange zest
3 teaspoons active dry yeast

Directions:
Place all ingredients in bread machine and push start. This is a small and more compact loaf.

* * GERMAN RYE BREAD

This dark, lush pumpernickel bread is just bursting with flavor from caraway, fennel, and rye. Add a slice of good Danish cheese and maybe a slab of Black Forest ham for an absolutely glorious combination of international flavors. Don't forget the icy mug of German beer to wash it all down!

Ingredients:

This makes a 1 1/2 pound loaf in a bread machine.

1 1/8 cups water
2 tablespoons cider vinegar
2 1/2 cups bread flour
1 cup rye flour
1 teaspoon salt
2 tablespoons butter or margarine
2 tablespoons dark corn syrup
1 tablespoon brown sugar
3 tablespoons cocoa powder
1 teaspoon instant coffee powder
1 tablespoon caraway seeds
1/4 teaspoon fennel seeds
2 teaspoons active dry yeast

Directions:

Place all ingredients into machine and push start. It will slice easier if you can wait for it to cool, but I never can. My slices are thick and jagged, but hot and delicious!

ANCIENT RECIPE FOR A PERFECT AFTERNOON!

"A book of verses underneath the bough, a jug of wine, a loaf of bread -- and thou . . . . "   Omar Khayyam

This sounds wonderful. The only thing missing is the cheese! The classic combination of bread, wine and cheese will indeed make for the perfect afternoon. Garnish with a few friends and enjoy!

Breads

* * * FRUIT & HONEY BREAD

This breakfast bread stays moist. It is as delicious the second day as it was the first. You might try raisins, figs, or peaches in place of the dates and apricots.

Ingredients:

1 3/4 cups all-purpose flour
1 cup graham cracker crumbs (about 14 squares)
1 1/2 teaspoons baking powder
2 eggs
1/2 cup honey
1/4 cup vegetable oil
1/4 cup orange juice
2 teaspoons grated orange zest
1 cup apple, chopped and peeled
1/2 cup chopped dates
1/2 cup chopped dried apricots

Directions:

In a large bowl, combine flour, crumbs and baking powder. In another bowl, beat eggs, honey, oil, orange juice, and zest. Stir into dry ingredients just until moistened. Fold in apple, dates, and apricots. Spoon into three greased 5 3/4 x 3 x 2 inch loaf pans. (or two 8 1/2 x 4 inch) Bake at 350 degrees for 45-50 minutes. Check at 40 minutes if using the larger pans. Breads are done when a toothpick inserted near the center comes out clean. Cool for 10 minutes before removing from pans. Transfer to wire racks to cool. Yields 2-3 loaves.

Breads

* * * NEW YORK APPLE MUFFINS

A simple confection brought to life with pungently fresh orange zest and toasted hazelnuts. All you need is one of these muffins and a steaming, freshly brewed cup of coffee and life is good.

Ingredients for muffins:

2 cups flour
1/2 cup sugar
1 tablespoon baking powder
1/2 teaspoon salt
1/2 cup cold butter
2 eggs, beaten
1/2 cup sour cream
3/4 cup milk
1 cup apple, peeled and diced

Directions for muffins:

Grease muffin tins and preheat oven to 425 degrees. Combine dry ingredients in large bowl. Cut butter into dry mixture with pastry blender until it has a grainy texture. Stir in apples. Mix eggs, sour cream, and milk together and fold into dry mixture. Fill muffin cups to about 2/3 full and bake for 15-20 minutes, or until muffins are golden brown and pass the toothpick test. Cool 10 minutes in pan and turn out onto rack.

Ingredients for glaze:

2 cups powdered sugar
3-4 tablespoons orange juice
1-2 teaspoons fresh orange zest, grated
1/2 cup hazelnuts, chopped and toasted

Directions for glaze:

Stir together powdered sugar, orange juice and zest. Adjust amount of orange juice to have a "drizzling" consistency. Glaze cooled muffins and garnish with orange zest and hazelnuts. I like lots of frosting!!
Yields 12 standard size muffins.

* * * DINNER ROLLS WITH ONION AND BACON

You can't beat the combination of onion and bacon in these tasty rolls. I like them best hot out of the oven, but they are delicious cold too. My husband likes to take these on early morning hunting trips. He says they make a great breakfast sandwich.

Ingredients:

1 loaf frozen bread dough, thawed
2 tablespoons butter
1/2 pound sliced peppered bacon, cooked crisp and crumbled
1/2 cup onion, chopped
Freshly ground black pepper
Grated cheddar cheese, optional
Freshly grated Parmesan cheese, optional

Directions:

Roll out dough on floured surface to about 1/4 inch thick. Using a 3 inch biscuit cutter, cut into pieces. I get 12-13. Crank some black pepper from your mill onto the dough circles. Stir bacon and onion together and divide evenly among the circles. Bring edges of circles together and pinch to seal. Place rolls in a 9-inch greased baking pan with pinched side up. Brush tops with butter and sprinkle with freshly ground black pepper. Let rise until doubled, about 30 minutes. Sprinkle the rolls with grated cheddar cheese or Parmesan before baking. Bake at 350 for 25-30 minutes or until golden brown. Warning!! These go fast. You should probably make a double batch. Also note that if you serve them before dinner, no one will have room for dinner. (But that is not a bad thing.) Yields 12-13 rolls.

Breads

* * * ROSEMARY & BLACK OLIVE SCONES

Savory, robust flavor from rosemary, onion, and black pepper abound in these tender scones. Serve warm with a tray of meats and cheeses or a steaming bowl of creamy chowder.

Ingredients:

1 1/2 cups all-purpose flour
1 cup rolled oats, uncooked
1 tablespoon granulated sugar
2 teaspoons baking powder
1 1/2 teaspoons chopped fresh rosemary or 1/2 teaspoon dried and crushed
  (The oils present in fresh create the best flavor.)
3/4 teaspoon freshly ground black pepper
1/2 teaspoon salt
1/2 cup butter or margarine, chilled
1/3 cup half and half
2 eggs, slightly beaten
1/3 cup finely chopped onion
1/4 cup pitted ripe olives, chopped

Directions:

Combine flour, oats, sugar, baking powder, rosemary, pepper and salt.

Cut in butter with pastry blender until mixture resembles coarse crumbs. Add half and half, eggs, chopped onion, and olives; mix just until moistened. Place dough onto lightly floured surface; knead about 10 times. Pat into 8 inch circle about 3/4 inch thick. Cut into wedges. Place in preheated 425 degree oven on greased baking sheet. Bake 18-20 minutes. Yields 6 scones.

Breads

* * * GRANOLA QUICK BREAD

Serve this bread warm out of the oven. If you are lucky enough to have some homemade apricot preserves to go along with it, you'll think you're in heaven. This is a great way to greet the day!

Ingredients:

1 3/4 cups flour
1 1/2 cups granola cereal (I used Northern Gold with blueberries.)
1/4 cup chopped dried apricots
1/4 cup dates or raisins
1/4 cup granulated sugar
1 1/2 teaspoons baking powder
1/4 teaspoon salt
1/2 cup milk
1/2 cup frozen orange juice concentrate, thawed
1/4 cup vegetable oil
1-2 tablespoons confectioner's sugar

Directions:

Mix together flour, cereal, dried fruit, sugar, baking powder, and salt.
In a separate bowl, blend milk with orange juice concentrate and oil. Stir together liquids and dry ingredients just until moistened. Lightly grease a baking sheet. With your hands, form the dough into an 8 inch circle , place on the baking sheet, and bake at 400 degrees for 20-25 minutes. Bread is done when a toothpick inserted near the center comes out clean. Sprinkle with confectioner's sugar, cut into wedges and serve. Serves 6.

Breads

* * * SAUSAGE HERB MUFFINS

Hungry? Have one. These are good anytime. The oniony snap of the chives and herbal green freshness of the parsley blend with the sausage and cheese to create a delicious brunch item or quick snack. Note: If you use hot Italian sausage like I do, it doesn't matter how snappy the chives are or how fresh the parsley is you won't taste it anyway. You may choose to use a milder sausage. Either way it will be delicious.

Ingredients:

1 pound bulk pork sausage (I like hot Italian.)
1 can 10 3/4 ounce condensed cheddar cheese soup, undiluted
1 cup shredded cheddar cheese
2/3 cup water
3 cups biscuit mix
1 tablespoon of fresh chives, chopped
2 teaspoons of fresh parsley, chopped (or more to taste)
Extra chives for garnish
Extra cheese for garnish

Directions:

Brown sausage and drain. In a bowl combine soup, cheese, water, chives, and parsley. Stir in biscuit mix until blended. Add sausage. Fill greased muffin cups 3/4 full. Sprinkle with additional cheddar cheese and snipped chives. Bake at 350 degrees for 25-30 minutes until brown and a toothpick comes out clean. Cool in pans 5 minutes. The biscuits need to set up a little bit. Then turn out to cool on wire racks. Yields 18 standard size muffins.

Breads

* * * GINGER SCONES

Is it chocolate and ginger or ginger and chocolate? Either way you put the two together; it's a great combination. Ginger adds a thrilling dimension to anything it touches. Scones are easy to make and these are a real taste treat.

Ingredients:

2 cups flour
1/4 cup sugar
1/4 cup brown sugar
1 1/2 teaspoons baking powder
1 teaspoon baking soda
1 teaspoon salt
6 tablespoons butter
1/2 cup buttermilk (I use powdered)*
1 egg lightly beaten
2 teaspoons pure vanilla extract
1/2 to 1 teaspoon freshly grated orange zest
5 ounces semisweet chocolate, chopped
1/4 cup crystallized ginger, finely chopped

Directions:

Combine flour, sugar, brown sugar, baking powder, soda, and salt in a large bowl. Cut in butter until mixture has texture of grain. In a separate bowl, mix thoroughly buttermilk, egg, vanilla, and zest. Add liquid ingredients to flour mixture. Stir gently just until dough is moistened and begins to cling together. Fold in chocolate and ginger. Preheat oven to 375 degrees. Drop 1/3 cupfuls of dough onto ungreased baking sheet. Bake 15-17 minutes or until golden. Cool on wire rack at least 5 minutes before removing from pan. Serves 6.

*If using powdered buttermilk, follow instructions on can for the substitution.

Martha's Cooking Tips for Eggs:

1. To make perfect hard-cooked eggs, place eggs in a single layer in a saucepan. Add water to come to at least one inch above eggs. Cover and quickly bring to a boil. Turn off heat. If necessary, remove pan from burner to prevent further boiling. Let eggs stand, covered in hot water 15-17 minutes, 3 minutes less for smaller eggs. Immediately run cold water over eggs or put them in ice water until completely cooled.

2. When cooking eggs, add salt last. It toughens eggs.

3. Egg shelf life is 10 days. A simple test is if the egg floats, throw it away.

4. To make boiled eggs easier to peel, add a teaspoon of salt or a tablespoon of vinegar to the water before cooking.

5. Adding 1/4 teaspoon cornstarch per egg makes scrambled eggs fluffier.

6. Adding 1 tablespoon of sour cream per egg makes scrambled eggs rich and creamy.

7. Use a funnel to separate whites and yolks of raw eggs.

HELPFUL HINT:

When preparing a new dish always read the entire recipe to make sure you have all of the ingredients and proper cookware <u>BEFORE YOU START</u>. There is nothing more frustrating than not having what you need at preparation time.

* * * ASPARAGUS PIE

Springtime fresh asparagus combined with the savoriness of thyme and sweet onions make this a succulent morning meal. The use of packaged pie crust makes preparation easy.

Ingredients:

1 1/2 pounds of fresh asparagus
1 package of refrigerated pie crust (I prefer Pillsbury)
1 tablespoon of butter or margarine
1 large sweet onion, chopped
2 tablespoons of Dijon mustard
1 cup of shredded cheddar cheese
1 cup of shredded Monterey-Jack cheese
1 1/2 cups half and half
1 teaspoon fresh thyme
2 large eggs
Salt and freshly ground black pepper to taste (about 1/4 teaspoon each)
1 cup of bacon fried crisp and crumbled (I prefer peppered bacon.)

Directions:

Wash and snap off tough ends of asparagus. Cook for about 30 seconds in boiling water. Drain and plunge into ice water. Set nine spears aside to use for topping. Coarsely chop remaining spears and set aside.

Unfold piecrusts and stack them on top of each other. On a lightly floured surface, roll them into a 14 inch circle. Fit into 11-inch tart pan, (a cast iron skillet works well also), trim extra dough off and line crust with foil. Put dried beans on the foil to keep the crust from puffing up. Bake at 425 degrees for 12 minutes. Remove beans and foil and continue baking for another 2 minutes, cool on a rack.

Sauté onion in butter until soft. Brush bottom and sides of crust with mustard. Sprinkle a layer of half of the cheeses on the crust followed by the chopped asparagus, onion, bacon, and remaining cheese. Arrange reserved asparagus spears on the cheese.

Whisk together half-and-half, eggs, salt, pepper, and thyme. Pour mixture evenly over the asparagus. Bake at 375 degrees for about 30 minutes or until set and golden. Let stand 15 minutes before cutting. Serves 6-8.

* * * CREAMY BAKED EGGS

Hard-cooked eggs never had it so good. They are baked in a creamy sauce full of mushrooms and cheese. This is a great busy day brunch dish because you prepare it a day ahead. Serve these eggs with thick slices of ham and fresh biscuits.

Ingredients:

8 hard-cooked eggs
3-4 tablespoons sour cream
2 teaspoons of prepared Dijon mustard
1/2 teaspoon salt
1/2 cup chopped onion
2 tablespoons butter or margarine
1 can cream of celery soup, undiluted
1 cup sour cream
1 cup button or brown crimini mushrooms--sliced
1/2 cup shredded cheddar cheese
Fresh chives for garnish
Paprika for garnish

Directions:

Slice eggs in half lengthwise. Remove yolks and set whites aside. Mash yolks with a fork or pastry blender, stir in 3-4 tablespoons sour cream, mustard, and salt. Mix well. Fill the egg whites and set aside. Sauté onion and mushrooms in small amount of butter. Add soup and one cup sour cream. Mix well. Pour half into ungreased 11 x 7 x 2 inch baking dish. Arrange stuffed eggs over the sauce. Spoon remaining sauce on top. Sprinkle with cheese, chives, and paprika. Cover and refrigerate overnight. Remove from the refrigerator 30 minutes before baking. Bake uncovered at 350 degrees for 25-30 minutes or until heated through. Serves 8.

Breakfast & Eggie Stuff

* * * BACON BREAKFAST BURRITOS

I never have any leftovers with this breakfast casserole. It's delish!!!

Ingredients:

10 slices of peppered bacon, fried crisp and crumbled
6 green onions, sliced
1 small can green chilies or 1/3 cup of chopped green pepper
1 garlic clove, minced
8 eggs
1/4 cup sour cream
1/2 cup shredded cheddar cheese, divided
1/2 cup Monterey Jack cheese, divided
3 tablespoons taco sauce
1 tablespoon butter or margarine
4 large flour tortillas
1 large tomato, chopped
Sour cream and taco sauce to serve with casserole
Fresh cilantro for garnish

Directions:

Cook bacon and drain on paper towel, reserve drippings. Sauté onions, green pepper (if using) and garlic in small amount of drippings just until tender; set aside and keep warm. In a separate bowl beat eggs and sour cream. Stir in 1/4 cup of each cheese, taco sauce, and green chilies (if using). Melt butter in skillet and add egg mixture. Cook over low heat, stirring occasionally until eggs are set. Remove from heat. Add crumbled bacon to eggs with onion mixture. Spray an 11 x 7 x 2 inch baking dish with cooking spray. Spread a small amount of taco sauce on the bottom. Spoon one fourth of the egg mixture down the center of each tortilla. Roll up and place seam side down in the baking dish. Sprinkle with remaining cheese and a little chopped cilantro. Bake at 350 degrees for 5 minutes or until cheese is melted. Serve with sour cream and taco sauce. Serves 4.

* * APPLE PUFF

This is great for breakfast or an afternoon snack. The aroma of sautéing apples with cinnamon and nutmeg is too hard to resist. I like to use a sweet-tart type apple for the best flavor. The appearance of this dish is fun too. It sort of puffs and fluffs out of the pan. Sprinkling it lightly with confectioner's sugar makes for a beautiful eye-catching presentation.

Ingredients:

4 tablespoons of butter or margarine
3-4 apples (depending on size) peeled, cored, and sliced
3 tablespoons fresh lemon juice
1/2 teaspoon cinnamon
1/4 cup sugar
3 eggs, lightly beaten
1/4 teaspoon salt
1/2 cup flour
1/2 cup milk
Fresh nutmeg
Pure maple syrup

Directions:

Melt butter in a large fry pan. Add apples and sauté until tender but firm inside. Add lemon juice, cinnamon, and sugar and stir together. In a separate bowl, mix together eggs, salt, flour, and milk; whip until smooth. If your frying pan has an oven proof handle, you can leave the apples in it for baking; otherwise, transfer them to a 9 x 13 inch buttered casserole dish. Sprinkle lightly with fresh ground nutmeg. Pour the milk mixture over the apples and bake in a preheated 425 degree oven for about 20 minutes, or until puffed and golden brown. Remove from oven and allow to cool slightly. Sprinkle with powdered sugar and serve. To make it a real dazzler, drizzle some pure maple syrup on a warmed serving plate and nestle the apple puff into it. Yield: 1 serving. Just give me a fork. (It will actually serve 4-6)

Breakfast & Eggie Stuff

* * * * MUSHROOM AND BACON BENEDICT

Okay! Let the feast begin! The eggs Benedict of all time! These little gems are flavor packed with mushrooms, spinach, bacon, and fresh tomatoes. They make the morning magic. Add a champagne cocktail with strawberries and a flower on the plate to create a feast for the eyes as well as the taste buds. (Okay, I wasn't going to say this. It's not lady like. But this dish is so good, it makes my palms sweat. I get the same feeling when approaching the shopping mall!)

Ingredients:

3 cups of assorted mushrooms (white, cremini, or shiitake) sliced
8 slices of peppered bacon, fried crisp and crumbled (reserve drippings)
3 tablespoons of shallots, minced; or green onions, sliced
5 tablespoons of bacon drippings or butter
Salt and freshly ground black pepper
8 ounces of fresh spinach, trimmed and cleaned (or pick up a bag of spinach salad already cleaned)
2 packages of béarnaise sauce mix (You could make it from scratch, but that's too much work for first thing in the morning. However, if you want to, the recipe is on the next page.)
3 tablespoons of fresh tomato, diced
8 poached eggs
4 English muffins, split and toasted
Fresh tarragon leaves to sprinkle over the top

Directions:

Make béarnaise sauce as directed on package, set aside, and keep warm. Fry bacon until crisp, remove from pan, drain on paper towels, and crumble. Sauté mushrooms and shallots in 3 tablespoons bacon drippings until tender, 2-3 minutes. Season with salt and pepper to taste. Sauté spinach just until limp in remaining drippings or butter, and toss gently. Stir tomatoes into the warm béarnaise sauce. Spoon some of the spinach and mushroom mixture on each muffin half. Top each with a poached egg. Spoon béarnaise sauce over each muffin. Serves 4-8.

To Poach Eggs:

In a deep 10-12 inch non-stick skillet, heat 2-3 inches of water to boiling. Reduce heat to keep water gently simmering. Break cold eggs, one at a time into a custard cup or saucer. Slip gently into water. Cook 3-5 minutes, depending on desired doneness. Lift out eggs with slotted spoon. Eggs can be kept warm in a shallow baking dish filled with warm water.

Note: A chilled 1998 Kiona Chenin Blanc was what I served with this the last time, and it was a great match.

* * * BÉARNAISE SAUCE

A classic French sauce that is velvety and tangy. It is as elegant and rich as they come. You can serve it with meat, fish, eggs, and vegetables. The packaged sauces stir up quick and easy, but if you would like to make one from scratch, here you go...

Ingredients:

1/4 cup of tarragon vinegar
1/4 cup dry white wine
4-6 tablespoons fresh tarragon, chopped
1/2 pound of butter, melted and kept warm
4 egg yolks
1 1/2 tablespoons shallot, finely chopped
1/2 teaspoon salt
1/2 teaspoon freshly ground black pepper

Directions:

Combine the vinegar, wine, shallot, salt, and pepper and cook until liquid is reduced by half. This could take about 5 minutes. You should have 1/4 cup of liquid. If not, add enough cold water so that you do. Whisk the egg yolks until very smooth. Whisk in the vinegar reduction and beat until frothy. Pour into the top half of a double boiler. Cook stirring constantly over boiling water until thickened. Remove from heat and continue stirring for a few seconds to make it smooth. You don't want any lumps. Pour in about 1/4 of the butter and whisk until smooth. Gradually pour in the rest of the butter, whisking constantly as you do. Whisk in the tarragon leaves. Adjust seasonings to taste. You may wish to add a little more vinegar for a tangier taste. Keep the sauce in a warm place. If it cools, it will separate. If it should separate, it can be brought back to a smooth consistency by stirring in a teaspoonful of boiling water, a small ice cube, or a teaspoonful of heavy cream.
Yields about 1 1/2 cups.

* * * FESTIVE FRITTATA

This colorful and vibrant frittata is a treat for the tummy. Purple, red, yellow, and green are festive colors of beautiful vegetables that are brimming with beautiful taste! Pair this with a fresh baked muffin for a real breakfast bonanza.

Ingredients:

3 cloves garlic, minced
1 large purple onion, sliced
2 red bell peppers, cut into thin strips
1 yellow bell pepper, cut into thin strips
3 tablespoons virgin olive oil, divided
2 yellow squash, thinly sliced
2 zucchini, thinly sliced
1/2 pound fresh mushrooms, sliced
6 large eggs
1/4 cup whipping cream
2-3 teaspoons salt
2 teaspoons freshly ground pepper
8 slices of bread cubed (I like potato or homemade pepper/onion bread)
1 8-ounce package of cream cheese, cubed
2 cups shredded Swiss cheese
Fresh chives and thyme

Directions:

Sauté garlic, onion, peppers, squash, zucchini, and mushrooms in olive oil until tender, drain on paper towels, pat dry and set aside. In a large bowl, whisk together eggs, whipping cream, salt and pepper. Stir in vegetables, half of bread cubes, cream cheese, and Swiss cheese. Press remaining bread cubes in bottom of a lightly greased 10-inch springform pan and place on a baking sheet. Pour vegetable mixture into pan. Bake at 325 degrees for 1 hour. Cover with aluminum foil after 45 minutes to prevent excessive browning. Serves 6-8.

Breakfast & Eggie Stuff

* * * HAM AND BROCCOLI BRUNCH PASTRY

This dish has a great presentation as well as a great taste! Simply bursting with fresh broccoli, ham and cheese--what a winner!!! When the last crumb is gone, your guests will be asking if that's all there is. The easy preparation is a real plus.

Ingredients:

2 8-ounce containers of refrigerated crescent roll dough.
2 1/4 cups of shredded Swiss cheese--set 1/4 cup aside for topping
1/2 cup or so of fully cooked ham, diced
2 1/4 cups of fresh broccoli, chopped
1 small onion, chopped
1/4 cup minced fresh parsley
2 tablespoons Dijon mustard
1 teaspoon lemon juice
1 tablespoon fresh chives, snipped
Freshly ground black pepper

Directions:

Unroll crescent roll dough and place triangles on a 12 inch pizza pan, forming a ring with pointed ends facing outer edge of pan and wide ends overlapping. Press wide ends together. Combine next 7 ingredients and spoon over wide ends. Remember to set some of the Swiss cheese aside for topping. Fold points over filling and tuck under wide ends. Lightly sprinkle the top with black pepper, chives, and remaining cheese. Bake at 375 degrees for 20-25 minutes or until golden brown. Serves 6-8.

Breakfast & Eggie Stuff

* * BAKED FRENCH TOAST

Gone are the days of mush. Bring on the syrup, 100% pure maple syrup! My-oh-my, there is a difference. Send your taste buds dancing and try some of this:

Ingredients:

10 slices of white or French bread, crust removed. Use enough bread to cover a
    9 x 13 inch casserole dish with two layers.
2 8-ounce packages of cream cheese, cubed
2 cups milk
12 eggs
1/2 cup 100% pure maple syrup
Garnish: toasted pecans or walnuts and fresh berries

Directions:

Layer 1/2 of bread in a 9 x 13 inch buttered casserole dish. Top with cheese and then the remainder of the bread. Mix together milk, eggs, and maple syrup. Pour over bread and refrigerate overnight. Bake at 350 degrees for 45 minutes. Top with powdered sugar. Serve with warm, pure, maple syrup. Toasted pecans or walnuts not only garnish, but also add a richness of flavor for that special touch. Serves 6.

Breakfast & Eggie Stuff

CHOCOLATE—SWEET, SEDUCTIVE, AND SMOOTH

Who can resist the decadent richness of great chocolate? Domestic or imported, light or dark--these are only two of the factors to consider in deciding what kind of chocolate to choose for baking treats or just eating for enjoyment. The flavor and texture of chocolate depends on the type of cacao beans blended and how long the chocolate is processed. Heating the chocolate and grinding it between rollers is called the conching process. The longer chocolate is conched, the smoother and more expensive it is. The cacao beans come from the evergreen cacao tree that grows in the tropics and is cultivated for its seeds (beans).

General Chocolate Information:

1. Unsweetened chocolate, sometimes called baking or bitter chocolate, is pure chocolate.

2. Unsweetened cocoa powder is pure chocolate with most of the cocoa butter removed. Some cocoa powders labeled Dutch-process or European-style have been treated to neutralize the naturally occurring acids. This gives the cocoa powder a more mellow flavor and a redder color.

3. Semisweet chocolate, sometimes called bittersweet chocolate, is pure chocolate with added cocoa butter and sugar.

4. Sweet baking chocolate is pure chocolate with added cocoa butter and sugar.

5. Milk chocolate is pure chocolate with added cocoa butter, sugar, and milk solids. Most milk chocolate contains less pure chocolate than semisweet or bittersweet chocolates, so the chocolate flavor is milder.

6. Quality chocolate is glossy, breaks with a snap and possesses a chocolaty aroma. Also, it will melt on your tongue without any waxiness.

7. Chocolate and cocoa powder should both be stored in a cool dry place, free of any moisture. Chocolate should not be frozen.

8. The classic companion for a chocolate dessert is, of course, a glass of red wine.

Chocolate

DESSERTS

* * CHOCOLATE NUT AND SPICE CAKE

This marvelously moist and chocolaty treat is just brimming with brandied fruit, nuts, and lots of spice which make it perfect for a brunch, an afternoon snack, or an evening dessert. Serve with the center filled with strawberries and mint leaves or flowers for a great presentation.

Ingredients for cake:

3 tablespoons brandy
3/4 cup chopped dates
3/4 cup raisins
1 box devil's food cake mix
1 cup chopped hazelnuts
3/4 cup coffee
1/3 cup vegetable oil
3 eggs
1/4 cup water
1 teaspoon ground cinnamon
1/4 teaspoon ground allspice

Directions for cake:

Place brandy, dates, and raisins in a small pan and bring to a boil. Remove from heat and soak for 20 minutes. Grease a 12-cup bundt pan and sprinkle with sugar.

Combine remaining ingredients in mixing bowl and beat with electric mixer 3 minutes or until well blended. Pour into prepared bundt pan. Bake at 350 degrees for 25-30 minutes or until wooden pick inserted in center comes out clean. Let cool in pan for 10 minutes. Invert on serving plate and cool. This cake doesn't need icing. However, if you like a little extra sweet, continue on...

Ingredients for Icing:

4 ounces cream cheese
2 tablespoons butter
1 tablespoon cream
1 teaspoon lemon juice
2 1/2 to 3 cups powdered sugar
Fresh orange zest for garnish

Directions for Icing:

Soften cream cheese and butter in microwave. Stir in cream and mix well. Add lemon juice and enough powdered sugar for desired consistency. Beat in electric mixer until smooth. Glaze cake and garnish with zest. Serves 18-24

Desserts

* * BAKED STRAWBERRY DESSERT

This recipe was created for my granddaughter Alexis. She loves strawberries and loves this yummy dessert.

Ingredients for filling:

6 cups strawberries, sliced
1/4 cup quick cooking tapioca
1 cup granulated sugar
2 teaspoons freshly grated orange zest

Directions for filling:

Mix all of the above together in a large bowl and let stand for 15 minutes. Heat strawberry mixture to boiling and pour into buttered 9 x 13 inch glass baking dish.

Ingredients for topping:

2 1/3 cups biscuit mix
3 tablespoons melted butter
3 tablespoons sugar
1/2 cup milk
2 teaspoons freshly grated orange zest

Directions for topping:

Mix topping ingredients together in bowl, just until moistened. Drop spoonfuls of batter onto hot berries. Sprinkle lightly with granulated sugar, freshly grated nutmeg, and cinnamon. Bake at 375 degrees for 50-60 minutes or until biscuits are golden and cooked through. Serve warm with whipped topping or French vanilla ice cream. Serves 8.

Desserts

* * * * CHOCOLATE CHUNK BISCOTTI

Biscotti is the ultimate cookie of choice for my Mom and Dad. They fight over these and have even been known to hide them from each other. Rich with two kinds of chocolate and toasted hazelnuts, these cookies are great by themselves, but are actually meant to be dipped into a steaming fresh cup of coffee. These cookies are a little more work but worth it!

Ingredients:

1/3 cup butter or margarine
2/3 cup sugar
1/4 cup unsweetended cocoa powder
2 teaspoons baking powder
2 eggs
1 3/4 cups flour
2 ounces white chocolate baking bar, coarsely chopped
2 ounces semisweet chocolate, chopped
1/2 cup toasted hazelnuts, chopped

Directions:

In large mixer bowl, beat butter or margarine until softened. Add sugar, cocoa powder, and baking powder; mix well. Beat in the eggs and then as much of the flour as you can. Stir in any remaining flour by hand, along with the nuts and both chocolates. Shape the dough into two 9 inch long logs. Place the logs onto a lightly greased cookie sheet and slightly flatten them to about 2 inches wide. Bake at 375 degrees for about 20 minutes, or until a toothpick inserted near the middle comes out clean. Allow the cookie logs to cool on the cookie sheet for about an hour.

Set the oven to 325 degrees. Slice the cookie logs into 1/2 inch slices on the diagonal. Lay the slices, cut side down, on an ungreased baking sheet. Bake them for 7 minutes, turn the cookies, and bake for 8 minutes longer. Cookies should be dry and crisp. Cool on wire rack. Yields about 32 cookies.

* * * * PETITS GATEAX

I was first introduced to these little delicacies when my daughter was taking high school French. She brought a recipe home and we tried it. It has since become a family favorite at holiday time. You can vary the color of the filling to suit the holiday or event you are celebrating. This is a great cookie to serve at weddings and showers. They are a melt-in-your-mouth morsel.

Ingredients for cookie:

1 cup butter
2 cups flour
1/3 cup whipping cream
Granulated sugar for coating cookies

Ingredients for cream filling:

1/4 cup butter, whipped
3/4 cup sifted confectioner's sugar
1 egg yolk
1 teaspoon pure vanilla extract
Color of choice (very lightly--the charm is in the pastel color)

Directions:

Mix butter, cream, and flour thoroughly. Chill for 1 hour. Heat oven to 375 degrees. Roll dough 1/8 inch thick on a floured board. Cut into 2 inch shapes (round works the best) and coat both sides with sugar. Place on an ungreased cookie sheet and prick with a fork. Cook 7-9 minutes or until slightly puffy. To assemble, put 2 cooled cookies together with cream filling.

These deliciously delicate cookies take a little time, but they are well worth the effort involved. They freeze well, so can be made in advance. Yields about 2 dozen.

Desserts

* * * BRANDIED APRICOT AND RAISIN COOKIES

This is a very rich dessert cookie that says "GOT COFFEE?" The brandy soaked apricots, raisins, and cranberries simply explode with flavor in this special bar cookie.

Ingredients:

1/3 cup golden raisins
1/3 cup dark raisins
1/3 cup snipped, dried apricots
1/3 cup dried cranberries
1/3 cup brandy (I use apricot. It is a good idea to keep a glass handy in case you need to check for quality. One can never be too careful.)
1 1/3 cups flour (divided)
1 1/3 cups brown sugar (divided)
1/3 cup soft butter
2 eggs
1 cup brown sugar
1 teaspoon pure vanilla
1/2 cup pecans
Confectioner's sugar

Directions:

Prepare a 9x9x2 inch baking pan by greasing it and then lining it with baking paper or waxed paper. This will make it easy to lift the cookies from the pan when done.

In a saucepan mix raisins, apricots, and cranberries. Add brandy and bring mixture to a boil. Remove from heat and let stand 20 minutes. Drain.

In a bowl, mix 1 cup flour and 1/3 cup brown sugar together. Cut in 1/3 cup softened butter. Press flour mixture into prepared pan. Bake at 350 degrees for 20 minutes. Whip 2 eggs about 4 minutes. Stir in 1 cup brown sugar, 1/3 cup flour, and 1 teaspoon vanilla. Stir in drained fruit and 1/2 cup pecans. Pour over crust and spread to cover. Bake 35-40 minutes. After 20 minutes, cover with foil to prevent over browning. Remove from oven and cool on wire rack. Gently lift paper around the edges to loosen the cookies and then lift them from the pan. Peel off paper. Cut into bars and sprinkle with confectioner's sugar. Yields 20 to 25 cookies.

* * * COCONUT CREAM PIE

Go ahead and indulge. The creamy richness of this dessert is worth every sumptuous calorie consumed.   The saying "LIFE IS TOO SHORT--EAT DESSERT FIRST" was created because of this pie.

Ingredients:

1 2/3 cups graham cracker crumbs
1/4 cup sugar
1/3 cup butter, melted
1 8-ounce package cream cheese, softened
1 cup cream of coconut (NOT coconut milk)
1 3.4-ounce package cheesecake instant pudding mix
1 6-ounce package sweetened flaked coconut
1 8-ounce container frozen whipped topping, thawed
1 cup whipping cream
Garnish: toasted coconut

Directions:

Stir together first 3 ingredients; press mixture evenly in bottom and up sides of 9 inch pie plate. Bake at 350 degrees for 8 minutes; remove to a wire rack and cool completely. Beat cheese and cream of coconut at medium speed with an electric mixer until smooth. Add pudding mix, beating until well blended.   Stir in coconut; fold in whipped topping.   Spread cheese mixture evenly into prepared crust; cover and chill 2 hours or until set. Beat whipping cream with an electric mixer until soft peaks form and spread evenly over top of pie. Garnish with toasted coconut. To toast coconut spread flaked coconut on a cookie sheet. Place sheet under the broiler and watch constantly. Stir coconut every few seconds to toast evenly. Remove from oven when lightly browned. Cool. Serves 8.

Desserts

* * * RASPBERRY CREAM PIE WITH PECAN TOPPING

Raspberries are the language of summer. Who can resist that distinctly intense sweet-tart taste of fresh raspberries? They are wonderful by themselves with just a kiss of cream or as in this pie--a true confection for a lover of raspberries.

Ingredients for pie:

1 cup sugar
1/3 cup all purpose flour
2 large eggs, beaten
1 1/3 cups sour cream
1 teaspoon vanilla
3 cups fresh raspberries (okay to use frozen if fresh are not available, thawed)
1 unbaked 9 inch pastry shell

Directions for pie:

Combine sugar, flour, eggs, sour cream, and vanilla in a large bowl. Stir until smooth. Fold in raspberries. Spoon into pie shell. Bake at 400 degrees 30-35 minutes or until center is set.

Ingredients for topping:

1/3 cup packed brown sugar
1/3 cup all purpose flour
1/3 cup chopped pecans
3 tablespoons of butter softened
Garnish: Whipped cream, fresh raspberries, mint leaves

Directions for topping:

Combine all ingredients and sprinkle over hot pie. Bake at 400 degrees for 10 minutes or until golden. Garnish with whipped cream, fresh raspberries and mint leaves. Serves 8.

* * * FRESH PEACH COBBLER

Beautiful fresh peaches that are dripping with juice and full of flavor are what you want for this recipe. Serve warm with vanilla bean ice cream and it's a great summer treat.

Ingredients for cobbler:

8 cups or so of fresh peaches, sliced
2 cups of granulated sugar
3 tablespoons of flour
1/2 teaspoon ground nutmeg
1 teaspoon almond extract
1/3 cup butter

Ingredients for pastry:

1 box of two ready made pastry sheets, or......

2 cups all purpose flour
1 teaspoon salt
2/3 cup plus 2 tablespoons shortening
4-5 tablespoons cold water

Directions for pastry:

Combine flour and salt; cut in shortening with pastry blender until mixture resembles coarse meal. Sprinkle cold water evenly over surface, stir with a fork until dry ingredients are moistened. Shape into a ball and chill (or open box of pastry sheets). Yield: Pastry for one double crust pie.

Directions for cobbler:

Combine peaches, sugar, nutmeg, and flour in large Dutch oven and set aside until syrup forms. Bring peach mixture to a boil, reduce heat to low, and cook 10 minutes. Remove from heat and add almond extract and butter. Stir until butter melts.

Roll half of pastry to 1/8-inch thickness on a lightly floured surface; cut into an 8-inch square. Spoon half of the peach mixture into a buttered 8-inch square baking dish and top with pastry. Bake at 425 degrees for 14 minutes or until lightly browned. Spoon remaining peaches over baked pastry square.

Roll remaining pastry to 1/8-inch thickness, and cut into 1-inch strips. Arrange strips in lattice design over peaches. Bake at 425 degrees for 15-18 minutes or until browned. Serves 8.

Desserts

* * LEMON CHIFFON

This lovely dessert is elegant in its simplicity. Fresh lemon zest and mint make this as refreshing in taste as it is pretty to look at.

Ingredients:

1 1/2 cups crushed graham crackers (about 18 squares)
1/3 cup sugar
1/2 cup melted butter

Filling:

1 3-ounce package lemon Jell-O
1 cup boiling water
1 8-ounce package cream cheese softened and
1 3-ounce package cream cheese softened
1 cup sugar
1 teaspoon vanilla extract
1 16-ounce carton frozen whipped topping, thawed.
Fresh mint leaves and lemon zest for garnish

Directions:

Combine the first three ingredients; set aside 2 tablespoons for topping. Press remaining crumbs onto the bottom of an ungreased 13x9x2 inch baking dish; set aside. In a bowl, dissolve Jell-O in boiling water; cool. In a mixing bowl, beat cream cheese and sugar. Add vanilla; mix well. Slowly add Jell-O until combined. Fold in whipped topping. Spoon over crust; sprinkle with reserved crumbs. Cover and refrigerate for 3 hours or until set. Garnish with fresh lemon zest. Can be made a day in advance. Instead of placing whole mint leaves on the dessert, cut them in a fine julienne and sprinkle on very lightly at time of serving. Serves 10.

Desserts

* * * BLUEBERRY PRESERVES COFFEE CAKE

This cake has a pretty presentation and a great taste. Moist and fruity with thick jammy bites of blueberries. From mid-morning brunch to late night snack and anything in between, this cake takes first prize. Bake and freeze for whenever you want to sneak a snack.

Ingredients:

2 cups flour
1 tablespoon baking powder
1/2 teaspoon salt
2 sticks unsalted butter, softened
1 1/2 cups granulated sugar
2 large eggs (room temperature is best) lightly beaten
1 cup sour cream
1 tablespoon pure vanilla extract
3/4 cup blueberry preserves for the cake
3 tablespoons blueberry preserves for the cake topping
Confectioners sugar for dusting

Directions:

Preheat oven to 350 degrees. Butter and flour a 10-inch bundt pan. Whisk together flour, baking powder, and salt in bowl. In mixer beat butter until creamy. Add the granulated sugar and beat until fluffy. Beat in eggs, sour cream, and vanilla. Add dry ingredients just until moistened. Spread all but 1/2 cup batter into the pan. Using the back of a spoon make a trench in the batter all the way around the pan. Mix the 3/4 cup blueberry preserves with the reserved batter and spoon it into the trench. Bake the cake for 50-60 minutes or until it pulls away from sides of pan and toothpick inserted in the middle comes out clean. Cool in pan for 15 minutes. Invert onto a wire rack, let cake cool completely, and sift confectioners sugar over the top. In a small saucepan, heat remaining 3 tablespoons of preserves and drizzle over the cake. Serves 10.

Desserts

* * CHERRY AND APPLE COFFEE CAKE

Delicious apples and sweet cherry pie filling combine with the full flavor of toasted walnuts for a great big taste sensation. This recipe is too good to be so easy!

Ingredients:

4-5 apples (Galas work really well.)
1 large can of cherry pie filling
1 box streusel type coffee cake mix (I used Krusteaz.)
1/2 cup oatmeal
1 cup walnuts, toasted
4 tablespoons of water

Directions:

Place apples in a buttered 9x13 inch glass baking dish. Pour cherry pie filling over apples. In bowl mix together coffee cake mix, streusel topping pouch, oatmeal, and nuts. Stir in water until mixture is crumbly and sprinkle over filling. Bake at 375 degrees 45-50 minutes or until filling starts to bubble and top is golden. Serves 10.

Serve warm from the oven and top with whipping cream or ice cream if desired.

* * * CHOCOLATE-PEANUT BUTTER CAKE SQUARES

You can't eat only one piece of this. Like a brownie only better, these cake squares have such a moist and soft texture that they beg to be eaten. Don't resist!!

Ingredients for cake:

2 cups of flour
2 cups of sugar
3 tablespoons cocoa (I like Droste but Hershey's is good too)
1 teaspoon baking soda
1 teaspoon pure vanilla extract
1/2 teaspoon salt
1/2 cup butter or margarine
1/2 cup shortening
2 eggs
1/2 cup buttermilk (I use the powdered because of shelf life)*
1 cup water

Ingredients for icing:

1/2 cup butter or margarine
3 tablespoons cocoa
1 teaspoon pure vanilla extract
6 tablespoons milk
16 ounces powdered sugar (1 box)
1 cup of chopped nuts--walnuts or pecans work best
3 tablespoons peanut butter

Directions:

CAKE: Mix flour, sugar, and salt in large bowl. Mix butter, water, shortening, and cocoa in saucepan and bring to a boil. Pour cocoa mixture over flour mixture and stir. In a separate bowl mix eggs, soda, buttermilk, and vanilla. Add to the first mixture. Bake in a large greased and floured sheet pan at 350 degrees for 25-30 minutes.

ICING: In saucepan over low heat, combine and melt but do not boil the butter, milk, and cocoa. Turn off heat, add remaining ingredients and stir well. Pour over cake while it is still warm. Serves 10.

*If using powdered buttermilk, follow instructions on can for substitution.

Desserts

* * * HERBED RIB EYE STEAKS

These juicy, tender, and flavor packed steaks have turned into a "Friday Favorite." Serve them with a baked Yukon Gold potato, salad, and a lush red wine.

Ingredients:

2 rib eye steaks 1–1 1/2 inches thick
1 cup of zesty Italian salad dressing for marinade base
3-4 fresh sage leaves, minced (or about a tablespoon of dried and crumbled)
3-4 fresh basil leaves, minced (or about 2 teaspoons of dried and crumbled)
2 tablespoons of fresh rosemary, minced (or about 1 tablespoon dried that has been ground up a little in a motor and pestle) Leave some pieces bigger.
4 teaspoons of minced garlic
1 tablespoon fresh parsley
2 capfuls of Allegro Marinade
Red wine--enough to sploosh on the meat and fill a glass for the cook
Freshly ground black pepper
Montreal steak seasoning

Directions:

Two to three hours before cooking, marinade meat. Lay steaks on a large platter. Pour half of salad dressing, Allegro Marinade, and wine on steak and pierce all over with a fork. Sprinkle half of all the seasonings on except for the Montreal and work it into the meat a little with your fork. Turn the steaks over and repeat using remaining half of above ingredients. Cover with plastic wrap and refrigerate, turning occasionally. Just before grilling sprinkle lightly with the Montreal Seasoning. This will add all the salt that you need. Preheat the grill to high. When the grill is ready, sear the steaks on both sides and turn the heat down to medium. Cook for 5-7 minutes on one side, flip them over and continue to cook for another 5 minutes for medium rare or longer to meet your preferred degree of doneness. Yields two wonderfully juicy rib eye steaks.

Note: The very best result is with fresh herbs, but the dried are still tasty. If you're not familiar with rosemary, start with a smaller amount. The pungent, piney flavor can be overpowering.

Meats

* * * * ROULADEN (Rendsrualaden) a German dish

My husband's family originally came from Russian Germany. This dish is from their heritage. The ingredients are unique and the flavors will awaken the taste buds.

Ingredients:

4 cups onions, sliced
1/4 cup vegetable oil
6 tip steaks (about 1/4 pounds each) pounded
Salt and freshly ground black pepper
Dijon-style mustard
6 slices bacon, partially cooked
6 dill pickle spears
Flour
3 cups mushrooms (button or brown crimini) sliced
2 teaspoons garlic, minced
2 tablespoons butter, divided
3 1/3 cups water
8 beef bouillon cubes
1 teaspoon thyme leaves dried or 2 teaspoons fresh
1 bay leaf
1 tablespoon flour
1/2 small package of fettuccine noodles
Fresh parsley

Directions:

In a large skillet, cook onions in 2 tablespoons of oil until tender, but not brown. Remove from skillet. Season steaks with salt and pepper; spread each with mustard, 1 slice of bacon, about 1/2 cup of onions, and 1 pickle spear. Roll up. Secure with toothpicks. They don't need to look perfect. They will taste great. Coat with flour. In same skillet, brown meat in remaining 2 tablespoons oil. In separate pan, sauté mushrooms and garlic in 1 tablespoon of butter and set aside. Add remaining ingredients except butter and flour to the pan with the meat. Stir in any onions that did not get rolled up in the meat bundles. Bring to a boil. Reduce heat and simmer 30 minutes or until meat is tender. Remove meat bundles to a serving tray and keep warm in the oven. Mix 1 tablespoon of softened butter with the flour. Stir into broth in skillet; simmer until slightly thickened. Stir in mushrooms. Remove toothpicks from bundles; serve with sauce over hot noodles. Garnish with fresh chopped parsley. Serves 6.

Meats

* * BRATZENBEEFENLOFE

The smoky flavor of the bratwurst really comes through and enhances the casserole. All you need is a salad to complete the meal. This makes great sandwiches, and the circles of bratwurst create a unique look when sliced. However, you won't have any leftover for sandwiches. It's too good!

Ingredients:

2 pounds ground sirloin
6 beef smoked bratwurst (fully cooked)
2 baked potatoes, shredded
1 cup sliced green onions
1 egg
1 teaspoon Montreal Seasoning, plus some for sprinkling on top
1/4 cup ketchup
1 capful Allegro Marinade
1 Walla Walla sweet onion, thickly sliced

Directions:

In a large bowl, combine all ingredients except Walla Walla sweet onion. Place mixture in 9x13 inch baking dish that has been coated with cooking spray. Prick bratwurst with a fork and nestle them into the beef mixture. Top casserole with thick slices of onion that have been separated into rings. Sprinkle with Montreal Seasoning. Bake at 350 degrees for 2 hours.
Serves 6.

Meats

* * BEEFINSAUZINBUN

This is my husband's favorite. These are quick, easy, and very tasty. I like to add a little punch with some crushed red pepper flakes. Toasted buns and lots of cheddar cheese round out a scrumptious weeknight meal.

Ingredients:

2 pounds ground sirloin
1 onion chopped
1/2 green bell pepper, chopped
1 clove garlic, minced
1/4 teaspoon crushed red pepper flakes
2 cups ketchup
4 tablespoons prepared mustard
2 tablespoons Worcestershire sauce
Salt to taste
Freshly ground black pepper to taste
1/2-1 cup water
2 cups grated cheddar cheese
3 green onion, sliced
Seeded hamburger buns, toasted

Directions:

Sauté ground sirloin, onion, green pepper, and garlic until meat is well browned. Add remaining ingredients. Simmer for 20 minutes or so. If mixture gets too thick, add a little more water. The longer it simmers the better the flavor. If you have the time, let it simmer longer--an hour is good. Spoon meat mixture onto toasted buns. Sprinkle with grated cheddar cheese and green onions if desired. Serves 4.

Meats

* * * * RACK OF LAMB WITH HERB CRUST

This recipe was inspired by Jerry Traunfeld, executive chef of The Herbfarm Restaurant. Lamb prepared in this manner is so juicy, tender, and succulent that it is absolutely the best ever. The flavors are intense. The secret is in the searing.

Ingredients for lamb:
2 racks of lamb, frenched and trimmed (about 2 1/2 pounds)
7 tablespoons finely chopped fresh parsley
1/4 cup finely chopped fresh rosemary, (could use dried, but fresh is best)
2 tablespoons fresh herbs (combination of thyme and sage or savory)
Salt and lots of freshly ground black pepper
3 tablespoons extra virgin olive oil

Ingredients for sauce:
1/2 cup full bodied red wine, (Cabernet Sauvignon or Merlot)
1 cup chicken stock
2 teaspoons of roasted garlic paste (roast garlic in oven ahead of time)
2 teaspoons of Dijon mustard
4 teaspoons balsamic vinegar

Directions for lamb:
Trim away any fat and remove the thin tough membrane. The top of the rib-eye should be completely bare but still attached to the bone. Mix all of the herbs together and firmly press the herbs into the racks, coating all sides of the exposed meat. Sprinkle any extra herbs over the meat. Wrap each rack in plastic wrap and refrigerate for 2-24 hours. The herbs are your marinade. Preheat the oven to 450 degrees. Unwrap lamb and season both sides with salt and pepper. Using a cast iron or other ovenproof skillet, heat oil over high heat until very hot and oil smokes steadily. With the top of the rib-eye facing down, sear lamb until the herbs turn a deep brown, about 3 minutes. Turn the racks over and put the pan in the oven. The underside will brown as they roast. Roast until a meat thermometer inserted in the center registers 120-125 degrees for medium-rare. (130-135 degrees for medium) This will take 10-15 minutes. Remove skillet from oven and put on stovetop. Remove racks from skillet, place on serving platter, and cover with foil.

Directions for sauce:
Drain oil from skillet, leaving browned herbs and meat bits in the pan. Remember that the skillet handle is very hot. It's a good idea to leave a pot holder on the handle as a reminder. Pour wine in skillet and heat over medium heat. Stir to deglaze pan. Whisk in stock, garlic, and mustard. Cook at a steady boil until sauce is reduced to 1/3 and lightly thickened. (4-5 minutes or so) Stir in balsamic vinegar. Taste and season with salt and freshly ground black pepper if desired. To Serve: Cut racks between ribs and top with sauce. Bon Appetit! Serves 4.

* ROASTED GARLIC PASTE

Roasted garlic has a nutty, mild and sweet taste. It can be used in mashed potatoes or spread on bread. It adds a mellow savoriness to meats, dips, and sauces. But above all else, be sure to have some on hand for the rack of lamb in herb crust!

Ingredients:
6 heads of garlic
1 tablespoon extra-virgin olive oil

Directions:
Preheat oven to 400 degrees. Cut top off of each head to expose cloves. Place heads on a large sheet of heavy duty foil and drizzle oil over cut surfaces. Loosely wrap foil around garlic to cover heads, but don't seal tightly. Bake until the heads are soft when squeezed and cut surfaces are nut brown, about 1 hour. After cooled, squeeze out the garlic and mash into a paste with a fork. The paste will keep (tightly covered) in the refrigerator for one week. Yields about 1 cup.

* * * *TERRIFIC TOURNEDOS

This is dynamic, a real show-stopper. Trust me, you will be using the slices of bread to soak up every bit of the sauce.

Ingredients:
1 pound of white mushrooms, sliced
1 1/2 sticks of butter
Salt
Freshly ground black pepper
1 tablespoon flour
1 cup warm cream
8 tournedos (slices of beef tenderloin cut 1 inch thick)
8 slices of French bread
1/2 cup of port wine (Definitely need a quality check here. Use a good port. This dish is worthy.)

Directions:
Sauté mushrooms in 1/2 stick of butter until liquid is evaporated. Sprinkle them with salt, pepper, and flour and blend well. Stir in cream and blend until smooth. Keep hot. Check the wine for quality and continue. Quickly sauté tournedos in 1/2 stick of melted butter, turning until they are brown but still rare inside. Sauté the slices of bread in the remaining 1/2 stick of butter, turning until they are evenly toasted. Put the tournedos on the bread and arrange in a ring on a heated platter. Pour mushrooms in the center. Make a sauce by stirring port into the juices in the pan. Season with salt and pepper and pour a spoonful over each tournedo. Serves 8.

Meats

* * * PEPPERED FLANK STEAK

A blue cheese sauce and lots of freshly ground black pepper, rosemary, and garlic make this dish a stand out. Serve it with crusty sourdough bread and a lush Pinot Noir.

Ingredients:

3 pounds flank steak
1/4 cup cracked black pepper
1/4 cup chopped garlic
6 bay leaves
1 tablespoon fresh chopped rosemary
3/4 cup Pinot Noir (Don't forget the quality check and be sure to fill your glass first!)
2 tablespoons olive oil
1 tablespoon red wine vinegar
1 cup beef stock
1/4 cup cornstarch
1/4 cup water
Salt and freshly ground black pepper to taste
2 cups of blue cheese, crumbled

Directions:

IMPORTANT allow 24 hours for marinade. Work black pepper and garlic into the meat. Place meat and next 7 ingredients into a ziplock bag and refrigerate for 24 hours, turning the meat 2-3 times during this period.

Remove the meat from the refrigerator 30 minutes prior to grilling. Remove it from the marinade and dry with paper towels. Strain the marinade into a saucepan, discard the herbs and spices and boil over medium heat until reduced by half. Add the beef stock to the simmering wine mixture. Mix the cornstarch with the water and whisk into simmering stock. Simmer until thickened about 7 minutes.

Season steak generously with salt and pepper. Grill 3 minutes on each side, then turn and cook 3 minutes on each side again for medium rare. Remove from grill and keep warm.

Remove sauce from the heat and stir in 1 1/2 cups crumbled blue cheese. Stir until smooth. Add more salt and pepper to taste. Cut steak into 1/4 inch thick diagonal slices. Serve topped with sauce and garnish with remaining blue cheese. Serves 6-8.

WINE SUGGESTION: 1996 Eola Hills Oak Grove Vineyards Pinot Noir

Meats

* * * * GLAZED AND STUFFED PORK LOIN ROAST

Brandy, apricot preserves, and spicy sausage really dress up a pork roast for a special event. I always make extra sauce to pour over the meat after it is sliced and to serve on the side.

Ingredients:

1 3-pound pork loin roast, boneless
1 pound hot Jimmy Dean bulk sausage
1/2 cup onion, chopped
1/2 cup seasoned bread crumbs
8 ounces dried apricots, chopped
Salt to taste
Freshly ground black pepper
Fresh rosemary, use dried if you don't have fresh
Fresh thyme, dried is okay here too
2 cloves of garlic minced or garlic powder
Alpine Touch Seasoning
1 8-ounce jar of apricot preserves, use 2 jars or one big one if you want more sauce.
1/2 cup sherry or brandy

Directions:

Mix together in large bowl the sausage, onion, chopped apricots, bread crumbs, and a sprinkle or so of salt. Slice roast down the center without cutting all the way through it and fill with stuffing mixture. Using kitchen string, tie the roast together as needed to secure stuffing (maybe 3 ties). Sprinkle seasoning to taste over top. I am very fond of rosemary and use quite a bit. If you are not used to the pungent herb, go lightly. It can be overwhelming.

Place meat in roasting pan to which you have added a little water. Cover with foil and bake at 250 degrees for 1 hour and 45 minutes. Add water as needed during roasting to prevent roast and glaze from burning. Mix preserves and brandy together to make glaze and pour it over the roast. Increase oven to 350 degrees and continue roasting for another 2 hours or until done. Check occasionally so that the glaze does not burn on the bottom of the pan. In a small saucepan, heat second jar of preserves and 2 tablespoons of brandy. Stir to combine. Remove from heat and set aside until serving time. When serving, drizzle some of the extra sauce over the sliced roast. Serve remaining sauce in a bowl on the side. Serves 10.

Meats

* * * PORK TENDERLOIN STIR-FRY

Wonderful is the only way to describe this spicy and juicy stir-fry. The first time that I made this dish, my husband and I would look at each other and say, "This is good, oh, this is really good" after each bite. We still do and you will too.

Ingredients:

1 1/4 pounds pork tenderloin
2 tablespoons soy sauce
1 tablespoon cornstarch
1/4 teaspoon salt
1/4 teaspoon sugar
1/2-1 teaspoon fresh gingerroot grated or use 1/4-1/2 teaspoon ground ginger
1/4 teaspoon cayenne pepper
1 medium onion, thinly sliced
1 medium carrot, julienned
1 garlic clove, minced
2 tablespoons vegetable oil
1 package frozen snow peas, thawed (6 ounces)
Hot cooked rice or angel hair pasta
Toasted sesame seeds, optional for garnish
Green onions, sliced, optional for garnish

Directions:

Cut the pork into 1/8-inch wide slices; cut each slice into 3-inch strips. In a bowl combine the soy sauce, cornstarch, salt, sugar, ginger, and cayenne. Add pork; toss to coat and set aside. In a large skillet, stir-fry onion, carrot, and garlic in oil until crisp-tender. Be careful not to overcook the veggies. Remove with a slotted spoon and keep warm. In the same skillet, stir-fry pork over medium-high heat until browned and no longer pink. Add onion mixture and peas; heat through. Serve over rice or pasta. Sprinkle with toasted sesame seeds and sliced green onions. Serves 4.

Meats

* * * * PORK RIBS POLYNESIAN

This has been a family favorite for many years. Thick and meaty country style ribs that are dripping with sauce and topped with pineapple simply disappear before your eyes. I like to bake them long enough so that the sauce thickens and begins to caramelize on the meat a little bit.

Ingredients:

4 pounds country style boneless pork ribs
1 13 1/2 ounce can pineapple chunks
1 cup ketchup
1/3 cup packed light brown sugar
Salt to taste
2 tablespoons of steak sauce
2 medium green peppers, cubed

Directions:

Preheat oven to 350 degrees. Allow 2-3 hrs. for ribs to cook. Drain pineapple, reserving 1/4 cup liquid. In small bowl, combine pineapple liquid, ketchup, brown sugar, salt, and steak sauce.

Coat a shallow open roasting pan with cooking spray. Place ribs in one layer; brush generously with half of sauce mixture. Bake 1 hour. Drain off fat. Turn ribs and brush with remaining sauce mixture. Bake 1 hour longer or until ribs are done and the sauce has started to brown and stick to the meat a bit. Top with pineapple chunks and green pepper 5-10 minutes before serving. Serves 4.

A simple side dish with this is white rice, sprinkled with peanuts, sliced green onions, and a little soy sauce.

PASTA

* * * * BAKED DEVIL'S PASTA

The heat's up a bit on this fiery dish. Just full of Italian sausage, garlic, red wine, rich cheese, and pungent fresh basil--you can't beat it! The pasta is baked in a rich red sauce and then topped with a béchamel sauce and Parmegiano Reggiano cheese.

Ingredients:
4 tablespoons of olive oil
4 garlic cloves, sliced
1 onion, chopped
1/4 teaspoon red pepper flakes
1 bay leaf
1 pound Italian sausage, casing removed and crumbled
1/2 cup red wine (A fruity Zinfandel works well, as long as it passes the cook's quality check.)
2 cups beef broth
2 1/2 cups of tomato sauce
3 tablespoons fresh basil, chopped (divided)
1 pound penne pasta
1 cup Romano cheese, grated
3 cups milk
3 tablespoons sweet butter
3 tablespoons flour
A pinch or two of ground nutmeg, fresh is best
1/2 to 1 cup grated Parmigiano Reggiano cheese (I like lots)

Directions:
In large sauté pan, cook in olive oil the garlic, onion, red pepper flakes, and bay leaf until garlic sizzles, about 2 minutes. Reduce heat to low, cover and cook until onions are soft. Add sausage to pan and cook over medium heat until sausage is well browned. Add wine and cook until most of it evaporates, stirring well to deglaze pan. Add beef stock and tomato sauce, bring to a boil. Reduce to a simmer, add 2 tablespoons basil and stir well. Simmer partially covered for 40-45 minutes, stirring every 10 minutes. Cook pasta until tender and drain. In large bowl, mix pasta with tomato sauce and Romano cheese. Pour pasta into ovenproof glass baking dish. In large saucepan, bring milk to a gentle boil. In separate pan make a roux with the flour and butter. Cook over medium heat until they form a paste. Add nutmeg to the milk. Add the milk to the roux a little at a time, whisking constantly to prevent lumps. Continue whisking until all milk has been added and the sauce thickens. Pour the béchamel sauce on top of the pasta and sprinkle with the Parmegiano Reggiano cheese. Broil for 3 minutes or until the cheese starts to brown. Then bake at 350 degrees for 10 minutes. Sprinkle with reserved tablespoon of fresh basil just before serving. Serves 6.

Wine Note: A 1995 BV Zinfandel, robust and fruity, was great with the spice in this dish.

* * * SPAGHETTI WITH BACON

Try this for something a little different. Sautéed bacon and onions float in a sauce of tomatoes and white wine. It goes together quickly and is absolutely wonderful. Don't forget the fresh Parmesan!

Ingredients:

2 tablespoons extra-virgin olive oil
1 cup lean bacon, cut into matchsticks
1 onion, finely chopped
1/2 cup dry white wine (Use a crystal glass for the quality check. It's important to make sure that the wine is not too dry.)
1 pound of tomatoes, fresh or canned, chopped *
1 teaspoon fresh thyme leaves
Salt and freshly ground black pepper
1 pound of spaghetti noodles
Parmesan cheese, freshly grated

Directions:

Sauté bacon and onion in oil until onion is golden and bacon is beginning to brown. (8-10 minutes) Add wine to the bacon mixture and cook until liquid boils off. Add tomatoes, thyme, salt and pepper. Cover and cook over moderate heat for 10-15 minutes. Bring large pot of water to a boil. Add salt to the water and stir in pasta. Cook until al dente. Drain, toss with the sauce and serve with the grated Parmesan. Serves 6.

* Note: If fresh tomatoes are not in season, you will have better flavor using canned.

* * * LINGUINE AND SHRIMP WITH GINGERED SAUCE

The first time I prepared and served this was to dinner guests. Yes, I was experimenting on friends again. The flavor is tremendous and the preparation is easy. The dish was a big hit and my dinner party a success!

Ingredients:

3/4 cup oriental sauce (I used Yoshida)
3/4 cup orange juice
3/4 cup honey
2 tablespoons fresh grated ginger
1/4 teaspoon red-pepper flakes
1 pound medium shrimp or prawns
  (shelled and deveined)
3/4-1 pound linguine pasta
2 tablespoons olive oil
6 green onions, diagonally cut into 1 inch pieces
1/4 pound fresh snow peas, trimmed
1 15-ounce can baby corn spears, drained, liquid reserved
3 tablespoons cornstarch
Freshly grated Parmesan cheese

Directions:

Combine oriental sauce, orange juice, honey, ginger, and red-pepper flakes in a small bowl. Pour 1/4 cup of mixture into heavy plastic bag. Add shrimp and marinate for 30 minutes, turning bag frequently. Reserve remaining mixture for sauce. Cook pasta until al dente. Heat 1 tablespoon olive oil in large skillet over medium heat. Add shrimp; sauté 2-3 minutes until golden and curled. Transfer to a large bowl and cover. Add green onions and snow peas to skillet and sauté 1-2 minutes longer. Add to shrimp. Whisk together reserved corn liquid and cornstarch in small bowl until cornstarch is completely dissolved. Pour into skillet. Bring to boiling; cook 1 minute. Stir in shrimp mixture with baby corn. Heat through. Drain pasta; turn into large bowl. Add shrimp with vegetables. Toss until well combined and serve immediately. Serve with fresh Parmesan. Serves 6.

Pasta

* * * FETTUCCINE TOSSED WITH CRAB AND ASPARAGUS

This is flavorful and light. Having the sweetness of Dungeness crab and the delicate taste of fresh asparagus, this is the perfect springtime pasta. Fresh herbs and lemon complement the dish and make it especially good!

Ingredients:

1 pound fettuccine (fresh pasta would be nice)
1/4 cup extra-virgin olive oil
3 tablespoons garlic, minced
1/2 teaspoon dried red pepper flakes
2 teaspoons grated lemon zest
2 cups dry white wine
2 tablespoons fresh lemon juice
1 pound fresh or frozen Dungeness crab meat
2 cups fresh asparagus, cut into 2 inch diagonal strips, lightly steamed
4 tablespoons mixed chopped fresh herbs (chives, basil, thyme, marjoram, parsley, or tarragon)
Salt and freshly ground black pepper to taste
1 1/2 cups freshly grated Parmesan cheese
Garnish with lemon wedges and fresh herb sprigs (parsley, tarragon, lemon thyme, chives, or lovage)

Directions:

In a large saucepan, heat olive oil and cook the garlic, red pepper flakes and lemon zest. Stir often for about 3-4 minutes or until the garlic is translucent. Add white wine and lemon juice, bring to a boil and then simmer to reduce the liquid by half. Meanwhile cook pasta until al dente and drain. Add cooked pasta, crab, asparagus, and fresh herbs to the garlic mixture. Cook stirring gently until just heated through. Salt and pepper to taste if desired. Serve immediately. Sprinkle with Parmesan and garnish with lemon and herbs. Serves 4.

Pasta

* * * FARFALLE WITH MUSHROOM SAUCE

EASY, EASY, EASY!! Using canned mushroom sauce makes it so easy. This is a mushroom lover's favorite. Lots of delicate mushrooms marry with Italian sausage and freshly grated Parmesan cheese to make even a simple weekday meal special.

Ingredients:

4 tablespoons of extra-virgin olive oil
1 onion, chopped
1 stalk celery, chopped
1 cup sliced mushrooms
5 Italian sausages, casings removed and crumbled
1 cup Chardonnay (Have your glass ready on the counter. Never miss a
   chance for a quality check.)
4 cups canned mushroom sauce
1 pound Farfalle pasta (bow tie)
1 cup Parmesan cheese, freshly grated
Fresh chives and/or parsley (minced) for garnish

Directions:

In large skillet, heat olive oil. Add onions, celery, and mushrooms. Cook until onions are tender. Add sausage and cook until browned and crusty. Add Chardonnay and cook until wine has been reduced by half. Scrape the bottom of the pan to loosen sausage bits. Add mushroom sauce, reduce heat, and simmer 25 minutes, stirring often.

Cook pasta until al dente. Drain and transfer to heated platter with high edge. Cover with sauce and mix. Toss with Parmesan cheese. Sprinkle with fresh herbs. Serves 6.

Pasta

* * * BAKED MACARONI WITH CHEESE

The classic comfort food. Nothing heals the soul like homemade macaroni with cheese. Béchamel sauce and piles of freshly grated Parmesan and cheddar cheese make this version outstandingly sumptuous. It will soon be your favorite.

Ingredients:

2 cups of milk
1 bay leaf
A pinch or two of freshly grated nutmeg
4 tablespoons of butter
1/3 cup flour
Salt and freshly ground black pepper
1 cup grated Parmesan cheese
1 1/2 cups grated cheddar cheese
1/3 cup bread crumbs
1 pound of macaroni

Directions:

In a small saucepan, heat milk with bay leaf. Do **NOT** let it boil. Melt the butter in a medium saucepan. Add the flour to the butter and mix well with a whisk. Cook 2-3 minutes. Stir constantly careful not to let it burn. Remove bay leaf from milk and gradually stir milk into butter mixture, stirring constantly until smooth. Bring the sauce to a boil and stir constantly for 5 minutes. Season with salt, pepper, and nutmeg. Add all but 2 tablespoons of the cheese and stir over low heat until it melts. Place a layer of plastic wrap right on the surface of the sauce to stop a skin from forming and set aside. Cook pasta in boiling water until al dente. Do not overcook as it will cook again when baking. Preheat oven to 400 degrees. Grease ovenproof dish and sprinkle with some bread crumbs. Drain pasta and combine with the sauce. Pour into prepared dish. Sprinkle the top with remaining bread crumbs and grated cheese. Bake for 20 minutes. Serves 6.

Pasta

* * * GOLDEN TURKEY BAKE

This dish is an outstanding way to use leftover turkey. When doing your shopping for Thanksgiving dinner, be sure to pick up any needed ingredients for this recipe also. Your family will love you for it. The savory richness of sharp cheddar cheese blends with the wonderful taste of toasted almonds. Fresh, juicy slices of tomato and a shower of fresh herbs, make this a truly delicious entrée.

Ingredients:

3 cups of turkey, cooked and chopped
1 1/2 cups celery, diced
1 1/2 cups sharp cheddar cheese, cubed
3/4 cup salad dressing (not mayonnaise)
1/4 cup sliced almonds, toasted
1/2 cup sweet onion, chopped
1 tablespoon lemon juice
1 teaspoon salt
Freshly ground black pepper to taste
1/2 cup bread crumbs
4 tablespoons butter, divided
1 tomato, sliced
Fresh herbs--parsley, chives, or basil

Directions:

Sauté celery and onions in 2 tablespoons of melted butter until crisp tender. In large bowl, combine turkey, cheese, salad dressing, toasted almonds, lemon juice, and salt. Stir in onion mixture. Spoon mixture into buttered 1 1/2 quart ovenproof baking dish. Toss bread crumbs with 2 tablespoons of melted butter and sprinkle over casserole. Bake at 325 degrees for 35 minutes. Top with tomato slices and sprinkle with additional grated cheese. Bake 5 minutes longer. Sprinkle with your choice of fresh herbs. Serves 6.

* * * * CORNISH GAME HENS WITH WINE AND TARRAGON SAUCE

Fresh French tarragon has turned into one of my favorite herbs. Tarragon is sweet and pungent at the same time, with an almost anise-like flavor. I usually use it with seafood, but in this case it makes the sauce and the birds "magnifique."

Ingredients:

4 cups Pinot Noir (that's about a bottle, less a glass for the cook)
2 medium onions, diced
2-3 carrots peeled and diced
2 celery stalks, diced
1/2 cup parsley leaves, chopped
5 fresh French tarragon sprigs
4-5 cloves of garlic, chopped
4 Cornish game hens
2 cups chicken stock
Salt
Freshly ground black pepper
3 tablespoons salted butter

Directions:

Combine the wine, onions, carrots, celery, parsley, tarragon, and garlic in a large bowl. Add the hens and marinate at least 2 hours. Large ziplock bags work well for this.

Pour the wine and veggies in a roasting pan or dish with a rack. Add chicken stock and set the hens on the rack (breast side down) over the wine mixture. Be sure to coat the rack and pan with cooking spray to make clean up easier. Sprinkle the hens with salt and pepper inside and out. Set roasting pan on a stove burner and bring to a boil over high heat. Immediately transfer to the oven and bake about 30 minutes. Turn the hens so the breast side is up and continue cooking until cooked through and evenly browned, about another 30 minutes. Use a thermometer to check degrees (185) for doneness. At this point the hens will have a nice shape for presentation on a plate. If you like the meat falling off the bones and into the sauce, then add 30 minutes or more to the cook time. Place hens on serving platter and cover with foil to keep warm.

SAUCE: Strain the pan contents into a medium saucepan through a sieve. Return the liquid to the pan and discard solids. Bring to a boil over high heat and cook until reduced to about 1 1/2 cups. This takes about 15 minutes, but it is worth it. Stir in the butter and pour over the hens. Serves 4.

Poultry

* * * TARRAGON CHICKEN IN CHAMPAGNE SAUCE

French tarragon, colorful grapes, and a bottle of bubbly make this a remarkable dish. The grapes don't add a lot of flavor, but they do make a beautiful presentation in a rich and creamy sauce.

Ingredients:

1/3 cup flour
1 teaspoon salt
1/4 teaspoon freshly ground black pepper
2 tablespoons vegetable oil
1-2 cups of champagne (The quality check is a must and my glass is ready!)
2-3 sprigs of fresh French tarragon
1 cup heavy cream
1/2 cup sour cream
1 cup of mixed green and red seedless grapes
6 boneless and skinless chicken breast halves

Directions:

Combine flour, salt, and pepper. Lightly dust the chicken breasts with the flour mixture. Reserve left over flour. Heat oil in skillet. Brown chicken about 2 minutes on each side. Add the champagne and tarragon. Cover and simmer the chicken 10-15 minutes or until juices run clear. Whisk together, heavy cream, sour cream, 2 tablespoons of the seasoned flour mixture until smooth. Remove chicken to serving platter and keep warm. Add cream mixture and grapes to the skillet. Stir constantly until sauce bubbles and thickens. Pour over chicken and serve. Garnish with fresh tarragon leaves. Serves 6.

Poultry

* * * * * ROAST DUCKLING WITH ORANGE SAUCE

My husband is an avid duck hunter. I have tried unsuccessfully over the years to prepare duck so that it doesn't taste like duck. I have found that there is a big difference between the flavor of wild duck and tame duck. The following recipe creates a fine, crisp skinned duck. You must start by purchasing a TAME duck from the grocery store. Do not shoot your own! Do not cook one that someone shot for you. My personal preference for the preparation of wild duck is to give it to the dog. It gives her something to bury, but I digress. The following recipe is simply delicious. The long roasting gets rid of the fat and produces a crisp-skinned, juicy bird that actually tastes a lot like pork roast. That's good duck! The sauce is the best part. It's absolutely oozing with flavors from blending oranges, currant jelly, and cognac. It's one you have to try.

Ingredients for duckling:
1 5-6 pound duckling
Salt and freshly ground black pepper
2 navel oranges, peeled, skinned and sliced thin

Directions for duckling:
Preheat oven to 400 degrees. Rub inside and out with salt and pepper, prick the skin all over with a fork, skewer the opening of the cavity and tie the legs together with kitchen string. Roast, breast down, on rack in shallow pan for 20 minutes. Reduce oven to 325 degrees. Turn duckling on its back and continue roasting for another hour or longer, until the crisp skin clings to the meat with no fat between them. Serve with sliced oranges over the duck and the orange sauce.

Ingredients for sauce:
Duck drippings
1 cup chicken broth
1/8 cup each sugar, water, and currant vinegar
Salt and freshly ground black pepper
2 tablespoons currant jelly
Juice from 2 oranges
Rind from one orange cut in a very fine julienne
1/2 teaspoon lemon juice
1/2 cup cognac

Directions for sauce:
When duck is nearly done, transfer to another pan and use roasting pan with drippings to make the sauce. Skim fat from pan and stir in chicken broth with duck juices, being careful to scrape any crusty bits from sides and bottom of the pan. Simmer, skimming surface as needed. In a small saucepan stir together sugar and water. Cook over medium heat until water evaporates and sugar caramelizes to a light brown. Add currant vinegar, salt, and pepper and cook until caramel is dissolved. Add the currant jelly, orange, lemon juice and the orange rind. Blend and add to the duck stock. Stir in cognac. Reduce a little more and pour over the duck. Serves 4.

Poultry

* * * CHILI STUFFED CHICKEN BREAST

Chicken boring? I don't think so! These zesty chicken rolls are terrific and easy to prepare. Ooey, gooey Monterey Jack cheese, green chilies, Parmesan cheese, and cumin are guaranteed to wake up any sleeping senses.

Ingredients:

6 boneless skinless chicken breast halves
6 ounces Monterey Jack cheese, cut into slices 2 inches long by 1/2 inch wide
2 cans (4 ounces each) green chilies, drained
1/2 cup Parmesan flavored bread crumbs
1/4 cup freshly grated Parmesan cheese
1 heaping tablespoon of chili powder
1/2 teaspoon salt
1/4-1/2 teaspoon ground cumin
3/4 cup all-purpose flour
1/2 cup melted butter
Garnish: freshly grated Parmesan, fresh cilantro, and fresh diced tomatoes

Directions:

Flatten chicken to 1/8 inch thickness. Place a cheese stick in the middle of each; top with chilies. Roll up and tuck in ends. Secure with toothpicks. In a shallow bowl, combine the bread crumbs, Parmesan cheese, chili powder, salt, and cumin. Coat chicken with flour, then dip in butter and roll in crumb mixture. Place chicken breasts seam side down in a greased 13x9 inch baking dish. Bake uncovered at 400 degrees for 25 minutes or until chicken juices run clear. Discard toothpicks prior to serving. Garnish with freshly grated Parmesan, cilantro and fresh chopped tomatoes. Serves 6.

* * * HONEY GRILLED CHICKEN WITH SWEET CHERRIES

Taste the flavor, taste the season! Fresh and juicy sweet cherries, a splash of red wine, and a summer evening on the deck are the perfect combination. Let the grilling begin! This simple dish is as beautiful as it is delicious. The honey brushed chicken turns a wonderful golden brown on the grill and is served with a deep ruby cherry sauce.

Ingredients for sauce:

1/3 cup dry, red wine
3 tablespoons brown sugar
2 tablespoons red wine vinegar
2 tablespoons orange juice
1/2 teaspoon grated orange rind
2 1/4 cups pitted and quartered sweet cherries
2 teaspoons cornstarch
2 teaspoons water

Directions for sauce:

Open the wine, take a wineglass from the shelf, fill it about half full and give it to the cook for quality check. (That could be you.) Combine 1/3 cup wine, brown sugar, vinegar, orange juice, and orange rind in saucepan. Bring to a boil and cook 5 minutes. Reduce heat and add cherries. Simmer 10 minutes, stirring occasionally. Combine cornstarch and water. Stir well and add to cherry mixture. Bring to a boil and cook one minute or until slightly thickened, stirring constantly. Pour into a bowl, set aside, and keep warm.

Ingredients for chicken:

6 chicken breast halves
2 tablespoons honey
2 tablespoons lemon juice
1/2 teaspoon salt
1/2 teaspoon freshly ground black pepper

Directions for chicken:

Combine honey and lemon juice. Stir well and set aside.

Sprinkle chicken with salt and pepper. Coat grill rack with cooking spray. Leave skin on chicken for grilling. It will stay moister. Brush chicken with 1/2 of honey mixture and place chicken on grill. Cook 25 minutes, turning every 5 minutes. Bush with remaining honey mixture. Cook another 5 minutes or until chicken is done. Serve with cherry sauce. Serves 6.

Poultry

RICE

* * WATER CHESTNUTS AND RICE

Elegant and delicious apply to this side dish. You have the perfect blend of creamy rice, crunchy water chestnuts, and richness of mushrooms. Serve this with any barbecue or steak. This is an easy "no fuss recipe."

Ingredients:

1/2 cup butter
1 cup raw rice
1 8-ounce can water chestnuts, liquid reserved
1 4-ounce can sliced mushrooms, liquid reserved
1 10 3/4-ounce can onion soup
2 tablespoons dried, chopped onions

Directions:

Melt butter. Sauté sliced mushrooms and water chestnuts in butter. Add can of onion soup. Pour reserved liquids into empty soup can and finish filling with water. Pour cup of rice into casserole. Add mixture and stir. Bake in preheated 300 degree oven for 1 hour in covered casserole. Serves 6.

* * HERBED RICE WITH TOMATOES AND BASIL

Garden fresh tomatoes and pungent, sweet basil are a must for the success of this side dish/salad. It is perfect in its simplicity. Serve hot or cold.

Ingredients:

3 cups of cooked rice
1 cup coarsely chopped tomatoes
1 tablespoon fresh herbs of choice*
1 tablespoon fresh chives, chopped
2 tablespoons torn basil leaves
1 teaspoon salt
Freshly ground black pepper to taste
Balsamic vinegar

Directions:

Combine all ingredients except vinegar, tossing gently. Drizzle with balsamic vinegar to taste. Serves 4.

 *Other fresh herb choices might be tarragon, parsley, lovage, or even the tanginess of sorrel to add fragrance, taste, and texture.

Rice

** RICE WITH GREEN PEPPERS AND ONIONS

This colorful casserole may become a family favorite. Easy to prepare and full of flavor from sweet green bell peppers, tender green onions, and fresh parsley.

Ingredients:
1 cup green onions, thinly sliced with tops
1/2 cup finely chopped green pepper
2 tablespoons butter
1 1/2 cups chicken broth
2/3 cups raw rice
1/4 cup fresh parsley, minced
Freshly ground black pepper
1/2 teaspoon salt
1/2 cup cheddar cheese, grated

Directions:
Sauté onions in butter in skillet until tender. Stir in broth, rice, green pepper, parsley, salt, and black pepper. Bring to a boil. Remove from heat and pour into a greased 1 quart baking dish. Cover and bake at 350 degrees for 25 minutes or until rice is tender. Sprinkle with cheese. Continue baking until cheese is melted, another 5 minutes or so. Serves 4.

* * * WILD RICE WITH SAUTED ALMONDS

Golden raisins add a touch of sweetness to this brown and wild rice pilaf. Serve it as a splendid side for ham or turkey.

Ingredients:
5 1/2 cups chicken broth, divided
1 cup golden raisins or chopped dates
6 tablespoons butter, divided
1 cup raw wild rice
1 cup raw brown rice
1 cup slivered almonds or pecans
1/2 cup fresh parsley, minced
1/2 teaspoon salt
1/2 teaspoon freshly ground black pepper

Directions:
Place raisins and 1/2 cup chicken broth in a small saucepan and bring to a boil. Remove from heat. In a large saucepan, bring 3 cups of broth and 2 tablespoons of butter to a boil. Add wild rice; cover and simmer for 1 to 1 1/2 hours or until rice is tender. In a separate saucepan, combine brown rice, 2 tablespoons butter and remaining broth. Bring to a boil. Cover and simmer for 40 minutes, until rice is tender. In a skillet, sauté the almonds in 2 tablespoons butter until lightly browned. In large serving bowl, combine rice mixtures, raisins, almonds, parsley, salt and pepper. Taste and adjust seasonings. Serves 10.

Rice

* * * RICE WITH TOMATOES AND BACON

Scrumptious peppered bacon sautéed until crisp and brown adds richness to this rice dish. Add a little hot sauce for pizzazz and you've got a very tasty treat.

Ingredients:
2 14 1/2-ounce cans chopped tomatoes, undrained
6 slices bacon
1 cup onion, chopped
1/2 cup celery, chopped
1/4 cup green bell pepper, chopped
2 cups raw long-grain rice
2 teaspoons salt
2 teaspoons sugar
1/2 teaspoon freshly ground black pepper
2 teaspoon hot sauce (I used a spicy, garlic pepper sauce.)
1 5.5-ounce can tomato juice
1 tablespoon fresh parsley, chopped

Directions:
Pour tomatoes into a large bowl and mash them. Cook bacon in skillet until crisp. Remove bacon, reserving 1 1/2 tablespoons drippings in skillet. Crumble bacon and set aside. Cook onion, celery and green pepper in bacon drippings until tender, stir in tomatoes, rice, and remaining ingredients. Cook mixture about 10 minutes. Transfer to buttered 3 quart baking dish. Bake covered at 350 degrees for 1 hour or until rice is tender. Uncover and sprinkle with grated cheddar cheese. Return to oven for 5 minutes or until cheese melts. Serves 8.

* * WILD RICE WITH SAUSAGE

Crusty brown sausages, fresh herbs and the deep flavor of wild rice come together for a delicious blend.

Ingredients:
1 8-ounce package wild rice
6 pork link sausages
1/4 cup onion, minced
1 teaspoon fresh thyme or 1/2 teaspoon dried
1 teaspoon fresh marjoram or 1/2 teaspoon dried
3 green onions, sliced

Directions:
Cook rice according to package directions. Cook sausages until well browned and crusty. Add the onion and sauté until tender. Drain off fat. Stir in thyme and marjoram. Add sausage and seasonings to the rice. Sprinkle with the green onions. Serves 6.

Rice

* * * CURRIED RICE

Zip, Zing, Bang! There is spice here! This rice dish incorporates carrots, curry, ginger, and peanuts for a complex and richly flavored addition to most any meal. It is especially good with curried chicken dishes. It's great all by itself!

Ingredients:

1/2 cup green onion, thinly sliced
1/2 cup shredded carrot
2 tablespoons butter
1 cup orange juice (good results with apple juice also)
1 cup water
1 cup raw long grain rice
1/2 cup golden raisins
1 tablespoon packed brown sugar
1/2 teaspoon salt
1/2 teaspoon curry powder
1/2 teaspoon freshly ground black pepper
1/4 teaspoon ground cinnamon
1/4 teaspoon ground ginger
1/4 cup chopped peanuts or cashews
Garnish: 1/4 cup green onion, sliced

Directions:

In medium saucepan, heat and cook 1/2 cup green onions and the carrots in melted butter until vegetables are crisp tender. Stir in the water, juice, rice, raisins, brown sugar, salt, curry powder, pepper, cinnamon, and ginger. Bring to a boil and then simmer covered for 30-40 minutes, or until the rice is tender and the liquid is absorbed. Depending on cookware and rice, it could take up to an hour for rice to be tender. This is another dish that is worth the wait. Just before serving, stir in the peanuts or cashews. Garnish with 1/4 cup green onions. Serves 4.

Rice

Basket of veggies

SALADS

* * * SPECIAL SALAD

Light, sweet cherries and mandarin oranges are mixed in a light custard and whipped cream. My-oh-my, this is special! This salad has to be made a day ahead which makes it one less thing to worry about the day of a special dinner.

Ingredients:

1 20 1/2-ounce can pineapple tidbits
3 egg yolks
2 tablespoons of sugar
1 tablespoon margarine or butter
1 16-ounce can pitted LIGHT sweet cherries
2 tablespoons white wine vinegar
2 small cans Mandarin oranges, drained
2 cups miniature marshmallows
1 cup whipping cream
Fresh mint leaves
Orange zest

Directions:

Drain pineapple reserving 2 tablespoons of juice. Combine reserved juice with egg yolks, sugar, vinegar, margarine, and a dash of salt. Cook in microwave for approximately 2 minutes stirring every 30 seconds until mixture coats a spoon, or cook in double boiler. You need to stir frequently so that custard is smooth and eggs don't curdle. This will make a very light custard. Cool. Combine fruits and marshmallows and gently mix with cooled custard. Whip cream and fold into fruit. Cover and chill for about 24 hours. Sprinkle with thinly sliced fresh mint and fresh orange zest. Serves 4.

* * * ORANGE & PEAR SALAD

This is a beautiful spring and summer salad. The vibrant colors of the oranges and the strawberries mixed with the creamy white of the pears are showcased by the bronze-red of the lettuce. Make the dressing early in the day so the flavors can blend.

Ingredients:

2 medium sized ripe pears, peeled
Lemon juice
1/2 cup sliced strawberries
2 medium oranges, peeled and sectioned
Red leaf lettuce
1 tablespoon sliced almonds, toasted (or Almond Accents)
Orange rind curls for garnish, optional
Strawberry fans for garnish, optional

Salad Directions:

Slice each pear into 10 lengthwise slices and sprinkle with lemon juice. Chill sliced pears, sliced strawberries and orange sections. Arrange fruit on 4 lettuce-lined salad plates. Drizzle salads with honey-orange dressing. Sprinkle with almonds. Garnish with orange rind curls and strawberry fans if desired. I like to add fresh nasturtium flowers just before serving. Serves 4.

To make the dressing:

3/4 cup honey
1/2 cup white wine vinegar
2 tablespoons Grand Marnier or other orange-flavored liqueur. I like to overflow my spoonfuls.
1/2 teaspoon ground allspice
1 teaspoon grated orange zest
1/4 teaspoon salt
1/4 teaspoon ground dry mustard

Combine all ingredients in a jar, cover tightly, and shake vigorously. Chill thoroughly. Shake well before serving. Serve any remaining dressing over salad greens or fresh fruit. Yield about 1 2/3 cups.

Salads

* * * FENNEL AND RED ONION SALAD

Fennel, often overlooked at the market, should be added to your shopping list. The fragrant, graceful greenery can be used as garnish or snipped and added to salads, casseroles, soups, and vegetables as a flavor enhancer. The bulb has a slightly sweet and mild flavor. It is even more delicate when cooked. The following recipe uses raw fennel and is decidedly delightful.

Ingredients:
1 1/2 ounces Jarlsberg cheese, cut into small cubes (about 1/2 cup)
2 fennel bulbs, cleaned and shredded (If you don't feel adventuresome enough to try the fennel, 1 1/2 cups of chopped celery works okay)
1 medium red onion, coarsely chopped
1 cup canned garbanzo beans, drained
2 tomatoes, seeded and diced
1 cucumber, peeled and diced
1/2 cup walnuts, finely chopped
4 tablespoons white wine vinegar
2 tablespoons fresh parsley, chopped
2 cloves garlic, minced
Freshly ground black pepper to taste

Instructions:
In a large mixing bowl, combine all ingredients. Let marinate in refrigerator 1/2 hour. Garnish salad plates with snipped fennel fronds. Serves 4.

* * RASPBERRY TOSSED SALAD

Crisp romaine lettuce and splendid fresh raspberries in all of their summer glory abound in this festive party salad. But don't wait for a party to partake of this beauty. It is fun and fast to make and the dressing is out of this world!

Ingredients:
8 cups of romaine lettuce, torn
1 cup fresh raspberries
1/2 cup sliced almonds, toasted
1/2 cup seedless raspberry jam
1/4 cup red raspberry vinegar (cider works okay too)
1/4 cup honey
2 tablespoons plus 2 teaspoons vegetable oil

Instructions:
In a large salad bowl combine the romaine lettuce, raspberries, and almonds. Combine the remaining ingredients in a medium sized bowl and whisk until smooth. Serve with salad. Serves 10.

Salads

* * * HEARTS OF PALM AND ASPARAGUS SALAD

Hearts of palm are the ivory colored, delicately flavored slender inner portion of the stem of the cabbage palm tree. I like to use them in hors d'oeuvres and salads. This pretty salad is dressed only in a balsamic vinaigrette and is a fun summer luncheon dish. Serve it with freshly grated Parmesan.

Ingredients:

1 pound fresh asparagus spears
1 can hearts of palm (14 ounce), drained and sliced
4 medium plum tomatoes, quartered lengthwise
1/2 cup balsamic vinaigrette*
6 Boston lettuce leaves to line salad plates
1/4 cup freshly grated Parmesan cheese
Freshly ground black pepper

Directions:

Snap off tough ends of asparagus. Steam in saucepan with water or in microwave until crisp-tender. Place asparagus, hearts of palm, and tomato in a shallow dish; add vinaigrette. Cover and marinate in refrigerator for 30 minutes. Drain vegetables, discarding vinaigrette. Arrange asparagus, hearts of palm and tomato on lettuce lined plates. Sprinkle with Parmesan cheese and pepper. Serves 6.

*The exquisite Italian balsamic vinegar is made from white Trebbiano grape juice. It gets its dark color and pungent sweetness from aging in barrels of various woods over a period of years.

Ingredients for vinaigrette:

1/3 cup balsamic vinegar
2/3 cup extra virgin olive oil
1 tablespoon fresh lime juice
1 teaspoon thyme leaves
1 teaspoon oregano leaves
Salt and freshly ground white or black pepper to taste

Directions:

Pour the vinegar into a small bowl. Whisk in the olive oil in a thin stream. Whisk in the lime juice, thyme, oregano, and season to taste with salt and pepper. Yields about 1 cup.

Salads

* * * HAM AND CHEDDAR PASTA TOSS

Strips of ham, chunks of cheese, and a handful of veggies make this the perfect picnic salad. Pasta Toss is a very tasty change from traditional potato or macaroni salad. Everyone loves it, although my grandson picks out the peas!

Ingredients:

1 1/2 cups uncooked rotini (You may want to use tri-color for fun.)
1/2 (10 ounce) package frozen peas
1 cup cooked ham, cut in julienne strips
1 cup cheddar cheese cubes
1/2 cup celery, chopped
1/2 cup ripe olives, sliced
3 green onions, chopped
1/3 cup mayonnaise
2 tablespoons red wine vinegar
1 tablespoon olive oil
1/4 teaspoon garlic powder
1/2 teaspoon freshly ground black pepper
Salt to taste
1/4 teaspoon fresh oregano or 1/8 teaspoon dried
1 4-ounce jar of pimentos, sliced and drained
Fresh basil leaves, torn

Directions:

Cook rotini as directed on package, drain, rinse with cold water, and drain again. Combine pasta, peas, ham, cheese, celery, olives, and onions in a large bowl and toss gently. Combine mayonnaise, vinegar, oil, garlic powder, pepper, and oregano in a small bowl; stir well. Add mayonnaise mixture to pasta mixture; toss to coat. Cover and chill. Stir in pimento and basil just before serving, taste and adjust seasonings. Salad may need more dressing if it sits overnight. The pasta tends to soak it up. Serves 6.

Salads

* * * * CHICKEN BLT SALAD

Salad for dinner? You bet! This BLT version is a great main dish. Use chicken breast that has been poached in broth and white wine with a shower of fresh herbs for extra tender and flavorful chunks of chicken. Make the dressing early in the day so it can chill and the flavors can meld.

Ingredients:

1/2 cup mayonnaise
1/4 cup bottled barbecue sauce
2 tablespoons grated onion
1 tablespoon lemon juice
1/2 teaspoon freshly ground black pepper
2 large tomatoes, chopped
8 cups torn leaf or iceberg lettuce
3 cups cooked chicken, cut in chunks (about 3 breast halves)*
10 slices peppered bacon, cooked and crumbled
2 hard cooked eggs, sliced
Garnish: green onions, chopped

Instructions:

Combine mayonnaise, barbecue sauce, grated onion, lemon juice, and pepper in a small bowl. Mix well. Cover and chill. Press chopped tomato between paper towels to remove excess moisture. Arrange lettuce on 4 salad plates. Top each with tomato and chicken. Just before serving, spoon dressing over salads; sprinkle with crumbled bacon and eggs. Garnish with green onions. Serves 4.

*Note: To poach chicken, place boneless, skinless chicken breasts in pan with 2 cups of chicken broth, 1/2 cup white wine, and a handful of herbs of choice. I like to use parsley, chives, tarragon, and basil. Bring to a boil, cover, and simmer for about 5-10 minutes or until juices run clear. This creates very tender and juicy meat.

Salads

SANDWICHES

* * * THE MARTHA BURGER

The sandwich section would not be complete without a Martha Burger. This version is on the zesty side. Everyone will be waiting, with plate in hand, in eager anticipation of their burger coming off the grill.

Ingredients:
1 pound of ground sirloin
1/3 cup dry bread crumbs
1/2 cup water
1 teaspoon instant au jus or beef bouillon
1 teaspoon lemon peel, grated
1 teaspoon lemon juice
1/2 teaspoon salt
1/2 teaspoon sage, ground
1/2 teaspoon ginger, ground
1/2 teaspoon freshly ground black pepper
2 dashes of hot pepper sauce or Mongolian fire oil
4 hamburger buns
4 slices of fresh tomato
4 fresh, crisp lettuce leaves
4 thick slices of sweet onion
4 slices of Monterey Jack cheese
Optional: ketchup, mustard, mayonnaise, relish, pickles, barbecue sauce

Directions:
Mix first eleven ingredients together and form into 4 patties. Grill, turning once until well done. (about 15 minutes)

Assembly:
Prepare hamburger bun with condiment of choice. Place burger, cheese, tomato, onion and lettuce on top of condiments. To make a true Martha Burger, keep layering until your burger is approximately 6-8 inches tall. Now, get the napkins ready, hang on, and take a bite--WOW! Serves 4.

* * * CHICKEN SANDWICH EXTRAVAGANZA

Chicken breasts and thickly sliced sweet onions that are grilled to perfection do indeed give birth to a sandwich extravaganza. The key word for success is fresh. Fresh tomato, fresh basil, fresh greens, fresh lime, fresh, fresh, fresh....this is great!

Ingredients:

1 large tomato, cut into 8 thin slices
1/4 cup fresh basil, chopped
1 large sweet onion, cut into 1/2 inch slices (You need 4 slices)
4 boneless, skinless chicken breast halves, pounded
1 garlic clove, halved
2 cups fresh greens (lettuce, arugula, or watercress)
4 teaspoons of fresh lime juice
Salt
Freshly ground black pepper
8 thick slices of whole grain bread or whole wheat sandwich rolls

Directions:

On a large platter, lay out tomato slices, sprinkle lightly with salt and pepper and top with chopped fresh basil. Let stand one hour at room temperature. On barbecue set at medium heat, grill onion until tender and golden, about 10 minutes per side. Separate the rings. Using a meat mallet, pound the chicken breast a little to even it out. Season the chicken with salt and pepper and grill until cooked through, about 5 minutes per side. Grill bread slices until lightly toasted. Rub one side of each bread slice with cut garlic clove. Place two slices of bread on each of 4 plates. Arrange greens on one slice of bread on each plate. Top with chicken, sprinkle with lime juice. Overlap 2 tomato slices on second bread slice on each plate. Top with onion rings. The presentation is beautiful and every delicious bite will tell you it was worth the effort. Serves 4.

Sandwiches

* * * PIZZA PUFF

Everybody, even the kids love this dish. I make it spicy with hot Italian sausage, peppers, and mushrooms. It's definitely one that you can play with the ingredients and use what your family likes. I love things that puff and fluff. They are fun to serve and fun to eat. I consider pizza a sandwich type thing but you need a fork for this one.

Ingredients:

1 1/2 pounds of hot Italian sausage
2 cloves garlic, minced
1 cup of sliced mushrooms
1 cup of green sweet pepper, chopped
1 cup onion, chopped
1 1.5-ounce package of spaghetti sauce mix
1/2 cup water
1 15-ounce can tomato sauce
1/2 teaspoon dried oregano or 1 teaspoon fresh
2 cups mozzarella cheese, grated
1 cup flour
1 cup milk
1/2 teaspoon dried thyme
1/2 teaspoon freshly ground black pepper
2 eggs, slightly beaten
1 tablespoon cooking oil
1/3 cup Parmesan cheese, grated

Directions:

Preheat oven to 400 degrees

IMPORTANT: 1-Use only large eggs. 2-The meat needs to be hot when pouring on the batter so it will puff.

Cook sausage, pepper, onions, garlic, and mushrooms until meat is well browned. Drain fat. Add tomato sauce, spaghetti sauce mix, water, and oregano to meat mixture and stir to mix well. Bring to a boil and remove from heat. Immediately spoon sauce into a 3-quart casserole and sprinkle with the mozzarella cheese. In large bowl, stir together flour, thyme, black pepper, milk, eggs, and oil. Pour this batter over the mozzarella cheese. Sprinkle with Parmesan cheese. Bake at 400 degrees about 25 minutes or until lightly browned and set. Serves 6.

* * * HIDE THE SALAMI

Salami loaf can be served as a sandwich or an appetizer. The aroma of baking bread and spicy salami is irresistible. This is a beautiful golden brown loaf with all of the goodies hidden inside.

Ingredients:

1/2 pound Genoa salami, thinly sliced
1/2 pound mozzarella cheese
1/4 cup black olives, pitted and chopped
1/4 cup olive oil
2 loaves of frozen bread dough, thawed
1 teaspoon fresh thyme leaves
1 teaspoon fresh oregano leaves
2 teaspoons fresh parsley, minced
1 tablespoon fresh chives, minced
1 tablespoon fresh basil, minced
Freshly ground black pepper

Directions:

Preheat oven to 350 degrees. With floured rolling pin, on a floured surface, roll out loaves of dough into two 16x8 inch (or close enough) rectangles. Sprinkle 1/2 of the fresh herbs onto the bread dough and lightly press it in. Layer half of the salami, cheese and olives on each rectangle leaving a 1/2 inch border on all sides.

Starting from the long side, roll side over. Continue to roll until all rolled up. Moisten edges with water to seal. It is important to pinch edges very tightly to seal so cheese doesn't seep out. Sprinkle remaining fresh herbs on top of loaf and lightly press into dough. Brush with olive oil. Place seam side down on greased baking sheet. Leave space between loaves. Bake at 350 degrees for 30-35 minutes or until golden and crusty. Remove from oven, sprinkle with freshly grated Parmesan cheese if desired. Allow to cool in pan on wire rack for at least 10 minutes before slicing so cheese can set up and slicing is easier. Serve with napkins, fresh fruit, and maybe some Chianti. Yields 2 loaves.

Sandwiches

* * * SPICY STEAK AND ONION SANDWICH

Make your man happy. Caramelized onions and sizzling slices of steak that are piled atop herbed and toasted hot Italian bread will definitely put a big smile on his face.

Ingredients:
1 pound flank steak (about)
3 tablespoons virgin olive oil
1 large onion, sliced
1 tablespoon red wine vinegar
1 teaspoon salt
Freshly ground black pepper
1/2 teaspoon sugar
2 teaspoons fresh oregano or 1 teaspoon dried
2 teaspoons fresh thyme or 1 teaspoon dried
6 lettuce leaves, romaine or red leaf
2 12-inch loaves of Italian bread with sesame seeds

Salsa:
1/2 cup tomato, diced
1/4 cup mayonnaise
2 tablespoons minced onion
2 tablespoons ketchup
1 tablespoon jalapeno pepper, minced
1 tablespoon fresh cilantro, chopped
2 teaspoons fresh lime juice
1/8 teaspoon salt

Directions:
First make the special salsa. This is where the spicy taste comes from. Mix all ingredients for salsa; chill covered until ready to use. Sauté onions in small amount of oil until tender. Add vinegar, 1/4 teaspoon salt, and sugar. Continue to cook until onion is brown and liquid has evaporated. Transfer onion to a bowl. Add about one tablespoon oil to the pan and add steak to skillet. Sprinkle steak with remaining salt and freshly ground black pepper. Cook over medium-high heat about 10 minutes, turning once. Transfer steak to cutting board. Cut steak across grain into 1/8 inch slices. Preheat oven to 400 degrees. Slice the loaves of bread in half lengthwise and again in half crosswise. Brush cut sides of bread with olive oil, sprinkle with oregano and thyme. Bake on baking sheet until toasted, about 5 minutes. Layer bottom halves of bread with lettuce, top with steak, onions and the special homemade salsa.

Serve with tomato slices sprinkled with fresh cilantro, jalapeno pepper rings, thick juicy slices of lime and a small, frosty-cold bucket filled with ice-covered bottles of Corona (or your beverage of choice). Serves 4.

Sandwiches

* * * CHICKEN SALAD BUNDLE

A sandwich like this one is fun because it is different and easy. Whether you choose to use pita bread or a tortilla to wrap it up, you have a very flavorful luncheon or lighter evening meal. I especially like the whole wheat tortillas.

Ingredients:

1/2 pound cooked chicken, shredded
2 plum tomatoes, sliced thin (seeded if you prefer)
2 green onions, chopped or sliced into thin strips
1/2 cup mozzarella cheese, grated
4 flour tortillas or use pita bread
Several leaves of mixed greens (romaine or red leaf lettuce, and/or spinach), torn
4 strips peppered bacon, crisp-cooked and drained
Bottled blue cheese salad dressing

Directions:

Divide all ingredients except dressing among 4 tortillas or fill pita pockets. Drizzle with salad dressing and serve immediately. Serves 4.

SEAFOOD

* * * SWORDFISH WITH SALSA

This mighty fish has a very rich and distinctive flavor with meat-like flesh. It is an excellent fish for barbecuing and with this fresh salsa is very, very good. The vibrant taste of fresh dill and lime juice make a great marinade.

Ingredients for fish:

4 swordfish steaks, about 6 ounces each
Salt
Freshly ground black pepper
2 tablespoons Dijon mustard (heaping)
2 garlic cloves, crushed
1/2 cup olive oil
Juice of 4 limes
1/4 cup soy sauce
1 teaspoon freshly ground pepper
1 tablespoon chopped fresh dill

Ingredients for salsa:

2 large tomatoes, peeled, seeded, and chopped
1 medium onion, finely chopped
1/2 cup fresh cilantro, chopped
1 teaspoon crushed red pepper flakes
1 teaspoon Cajun-garlic hot sauce
Juice of 2 limes
Salt
1 teaspoon Cajun powder seasoning

Directions for salsa:

Combine tomatoes, onion, cilantro, red pepper flakes, hot sauce, lime juice, salt to taste, and Cajun powder. Stir well. Cover and refrigerate for at least 2 hours. It will keep for several days.

Directions for fish:

Trim fish and season with salt and pepper. Place in glass baking dish in a single layer. Combine mustard, garlic, olive oil, lime juice, soy sauce, pepper and dill. Mix well and pour over fish. Marinate in refrigerator for at least 2 hours. You will get the best flavor if you leave it overnight. Turn fish over occasionally. So set your alarm to get up every 2 hours. (Just kidding.) Grill about 4 minutes per side. Fish should be firm to the touch and flake easily when done.   Serve with fresh salsa. Garnish plate with fresh dill and cilantro. Serves 4.

* * * * CLAMS IN THAI BROTH

A recipe for the adventuresome! There is a little bit of everything in here. It's a really unique way to serve clams. I turn up the heat. You may want to decrease the red curry paste.

Ingredients:

2 teaspoons vegetable oil
1 teaspoon toasted sesame oil
1 tablespoon minced fresh ginger
2 teaspoons minced fresh garlic
1 tablespoon lemon thyme
1/2 cup coconut milk
4 teaspoons soy sauce
2 teaspoons Thai red curry paste (If you don't care for very hot, only use 1.)
1 teaspoon sugar
1 tablespoon fresh lime juice
1/2 cup clam juice
2 pounds fresh clams in the shell, washed
1/2 cup carrots, cut into matchsticks
1/2 cup red bell peppers, cut into matchsticks
1/2 cup green onion, cut into thin strips
2 tablespoons fresh cilantro, chopped
1 lime, cut into wedges for squeezing over clams

Directions:

In a large soup pot, heat oils. Add ginger, garlic, and thyme. Sauté for just a few seconds to heat through. Add coconut milk, soy sauce, curry paste, sugar, lime, and clam juice. Bring to a boil and immediately add the clams, carrots, bell pepper, and green onion. Cover and steam in the broth just until the clams open, maybe 5 minutes. Divide clams, vegetables, and broth among bowls. Sprinkle with cilantro and serve with lime wedges. Serves 4.

* * * * CHRISTMAS LOBSTER

It's hard to believe that lobster was once used as fish bait. This king of the crustaceans has become a Christmas Eve dinner tradition for our family. Tender, sweet lobster tail meat is combined with a béchamel and white wine sauce. The lobster is then spooned back into shiny shells that have been heated in butter. Ohmigod this is good stuff!!

Ingredients:
3 quarts water
1 onion quartered
2 whole cloves
1/2 cup sliced celery
1 bay leaf
6 frozen lobster tails (8-10 ounces each), thawed
3/4 cup butter
2 shallots, minced or 3 green onions, sliced
1 cup dry white wine (It is once again quality check time. You wouldn't want to ruin Christmas Eve dinner because you neglected to quality check the wine. I use a large glass because it is the holiday season.)
1/3 cup flour
1 1/2 cups milk
1/2 teaspoon salt
1/2 teaspoon freshly ground black pepper
1/4 teaspoon nutmeg, fresh grated is best
2 sprigs of fresh French tarragon, or 1 teaspoon of dried
Grated Parmesan cheese
3 fresh mushrooms sliced
1 tablespoon melted butter

Directions:
Pour water into a pan large enough to hold the lobster tails. Stick the cloves into the onion and add to the water along with the celery and the bay leaf. Bring to a boil. Add the lobster and bring to a boil again; skim off foam, simmer until tender, about 7 minutes. Remove from heat, drain and cool. When cool enough to handle, use scissors to cut the underside of the shell and pull it off. Remove lobster meat and cut into bite sized chunks. Dry the shells with a paper towel. Melt 1/2 cup butter in a large frying pan and heat the shells in it for a minute or two. It makes the shells shiny and pretty. Place the shells in a shallow baking pan and fan out the tails. Put chunked lobster meat in remaining butter and sauté lightly. Pour in the wine and tarragon and allow to cook down slightly. Set aside this while you prepare the béchamel sauce. In a large saucepan, melt remaining 1/4 cup butter and blend in flour to make a roux. Blend in milk, salt, pepper, and nutmeg. Stir constantly so you have a nice smooth sauce. Pour sauce over lobster and wine and mix. Spoon into shells. Sprinkle with grated cheese. Dip mushroom slices in melted butter and place 2-3 on top of stuffed tails. Bake at 350 degrees for 10 minutes or until hot. Serves 6.

Seafood

* * * SCALLOPS IN CREAMY GINGER SAUCE

The pungent and spicy fresh gingerroot is a remarkable companion for the tender sweetness of bay or sea scallops. This creamy, rich dish is absolutely wonderful served in puff pastry or over angel hair pasta. Fresh scallops should be pale beige to creamy pink in color. If they are stark white, then they have been soaked in water to add weight for marketing purposes.

Ingredients:

1/3 cup green onions, finely chopped
3 tablespoons butter
1 1/2 cups carrots, cut julienne
1/2 cup good quality dry white wine (Quality check required so have your glass ready.)
1 tablespoon fresh gingerroot, grated
3/4 cup heavy whipping cream
1/2 teaspoon salt
1/2 teaspoon freshly ground black pepper
1 pound sea scallops (Sometimes the bay scallops are sweeter, but I like the size of the sea scallops.)

Directions:

First pour a glass of the wine for yourself for quality check purposes. Sample the wine, and if acceptable proceed with the dish. If not, get another bottle and try again. In a large skillet, sauté the green onions in 3 tablespoons melted butter for about a minute. Add carrots and cook for 2 minutes longer. Stir in the wine, and gingerroot and stir until heated through. Add the cream, salt and pepper. Continue to stir until sauce is reduced by half. This could take 5 minutes or so. Stir in the sea scallops and continue to cook for only 2 minutes. They will get tough if overcooked. By this time you should be ready for another glass of wine with dinner! Isn't this fun! Serves 4.

Seafood

* * SCALLOPED OYSTERS

We love oysters. In this recipe, fresh oysters bake in crisp, buttery cracker crumbs. It is a seafood treat. But I have to wonder who was so brave to eat the first oyster and discovered that it was indeed a tasty morsel.

Ingredients:

1 1/2 cups salted soda cracker crumbs, divided
3/4 cup butter, melted and divided
20-24 fresh oysters or 2 12-ounce jars of Pacific oysters
Salt
Freshly ground black pepper
Ground red pepper (cayenne)
Fresh chives, snipped
Garnish: fresh lemon slices

Directions:

Preheat oven to 400 degrees. Butter a shallow baking dish 12 inch in diameter. Spread 3/4 cup of cracker crumbs over the bottom of the baking dish. Put oysters in 1/2 cup of the melted butter. Arrange in a single layer on top of the cracker crumbs. Drizzle with remaining butter in pan. Sprinkle with salt, freshly ground pepper, and red pepper to taste. Top with remaining cracker crumbs. Drizzle remaining 1/4 cup of melted butter over the crumbs. Sprinkle with snipped chives. Place baking dish on oven rack near top of the oven. Bake uncovered for about 15 minutes or until crumbs are well browned. Serves 4.

* ZESTY DILL SAUCE

This is a sauce that is good for seafood and vegetables.

Ingredients:

1/2 cup sour cream
2 tablespoons mayonnaise
2 green onions finely chopped
4 tablespoons fresh dill, chopped
2 teaspoons Dijon mustard
Grated zest of 1 lemon

Directions:

Combine all ingredients and chill until ready to use. Yields about 1 cup.

** SALMON IN LEMON CREAM

Sometimes simplicity when cooking fish is the best. Salmon is an excellent fish for baking. This thick lemon cream sauce compliments the rich and mild taste of fresh salmon.

Ingredients:

4 salmon steaks
5 teaspoons fresh lemon juice
1 cup heavy cream
1 tablespoon minced onion
1/4 teaspoon salt
Freshly ground black pepper
Fresh parsley for garnish
Fresh chives, snipped
2 lemons, cut into wedges

Directions:

Preheat oven to 400 degrees.

Place salmon steaks in buttered baking dish. Combine lemon juice, cream, onion, salt, and pepper. Pour mixture over salmon. Bake, uncovered, for about 25 minutes or until fish flakes. Serve with some of the thick cream sauce spooned over each steak. Sprinkle with chives and garnish with parsley and lemon wedges. Serves 4.

** CUCUMBER SAUCE

This is a really good dipping sauce for deep fried appetizers such as zucchini, chicken wings, oysters, shrimp, and clams.

Ingredients:

3 long cucumbers
2 teaspoons salt
1 cup sour cream
1 cup mayonnaise
1 tablespoon chopped fresh dill

Directions:

Peel the cucumbers, split into quarters and discard seeds. Finely chop, sprinkle with 2 teaspoons of salt, and chill for at least 2 hours. Drain well. Mix with sour cream, mayonnaise, and dill. Let chill until ready to use. Yields about 4 cups.

SOUPS - STEWS & CHILI

* * * * CREAMY VEGETABLE CHOWDER or EASTER SOUP

Easter weekend has come and gone. I have lots of leftovers so I make soup. This is a delicious light, creamy soup with a hint of tarragon, ham, and fresh vegetables. A very nice springtime-type soup.

Ingredients:
1/4 cup butter, melted
1 Mayan sweet onion, chopped
3 cups celery, chopped
1/8 cup green bell pepper, chopped
1 cup asparagus tips
2 cups broccoli florets, chopped
1 cup baby carrots, julienne sliced
2 ham slices (cooked), diced
1 tomato, peeled and chopped
6 chicken bouillon cubes
6 cups water
1/2 cup fresh chives, chopped
2 teaspoons garlic, chopped
1/2 cup cream
1 1/2 cups milk
1 teaspoon dried basil or 2 teaspoons fresh, chopped
1/4 teaspoon dried thyme or 1/2 teaspoon fresh
1 tablespoon dried parsley or 2 tablespoons of fresh, finely chopped
Salt and freshly ground black pepper to taste (I like lots of pepper.)
1 teaspoon dried tarragon, or 2 teaspoons fresh (This is great stuff.)
8 ounces cream cheese, softened
Cheddar cheese, grated for garnish

Directions:
Sauté onion and celery in butter to soften. Add green bell pepper, asparagus, broccoli, carrots, ham, tomato, garlic, bouillon, and water. Bring to a boil and simmer 30 minutes. Add chives, basil, thyme, parsley, salt, pepper, and tarragon. Make a roux out of 1 tablespoon butter and 2 tablespoons flour. Cook flour until golden--about a minute. Very gradually stir in milk stirring constantly until mixture is smooth. Stir the cream and milk mixture into soup and heat through. Do not boil. Garnish with grated cheddar cheese and chopped chives.

Serves 6

* * * * ITALIAN SAUSAGE MEATBALL STEW

Here it is!! Lots of spice! Lots of herbs! A soup of soups, but not really a soup. This thick, rich, and meaty dish is a taste sensation! I think a hearty red wine is a great garnish for it.

Ingredients:

Meatballs:
1 pound hot Italian sausage
1 pound mild Italian sausage
2 tablespoons chopped fresh parsley
1 tablespoon chopped fresh cilantro or 1/2 tablespoon ground coriander
1/2 teaspoon ground cumin seed
1 small onion, grated or minced
1/4 teaspoon cayenne pepper
Olive oil for browning the meatballs
1/2 cup red wine

Sauce:
2 medium onions, chopped
1 small bunch of fresh parsley, chopped
2 pounds fresh tomatoes, peeled, seeded and chopped. If fresh are not in season and flavorful, you are better to get canned tomatoes than to use hot house grown.
1 teaspoon ground cumin
1 teaspoon freshly ground black pepper
2 garlic cloves, chopped
1/4 teaspoon cayenne pepper
1 tablespoon fresh basil, chopped
1 tablespoon fresh thyme

Directions:

In a large bowl, combine all of the meatball ingredients except the oil. Form meat mixture into 1 inch balls. Heat oil in skillet and brown meatballs on all sides until they leave brown crunchies on the skillet bottom. Remove from pan, drain on paper towels and set aside. Deglaze the pan with the red wine after you have tried a glass to make sure the bottle didn't have a bad cork. Add all sauce ingredients to the skillet except basil. Cook uncovered 30 minutes or until the sauce has reduced to a thick gravy. Return the meatballs to the sauce, add the basil, and cook together for 10 minutes. Serve over noodles. A little fresh chopped parsley or basil would be nice sprinkled over the top just for color. Serves 6.

* * * * CHICKEN JALAPENO CORN CHOWDER

As soon as the fresh local corn is available, we get the kettle out. Our Yakima Valley grows the best sweet corn and this chowder is the best because of it. Jalapeno chilies, known as chipotles in their dried form, give the zip and zing. The chicken and potatoes add the balance. Use Yukon Gold potatoes if you can. They are sweet and creamy. This chowder is not hard to fix, but it does take time to chop everything. Get Hubby in the kitchen to help. Mine is great in the kitchen and he keeps my wine glass full!!!

Ingredients:
2 tablespoons of olive oil
2 cloves garlic, minced
1 large onion, chopped
1/2 teaspoon ground cumin
1 teaspoon fresh oregano, chopped
1/3-1/2 cup jalapeno chilies, stemmed, seeded & minced
1 large sweet red pepper, seeded and diced
2 tablespoons flour
1 quart chicken broth
1 large Yukon Gold potato, cubed
2 large ears corn, husked and cut off the cob
1/2 cup whipping cream
2 chicken breast halves, cooked and cut into chunks **
Salt
Freshly ground black pepper
Fresh cilantro, chopped
1 cup shredded cheddar or jalapeno cheese

Directions:
In soup kettle, combine oil, garlic, onion, cumin, oregano, chilies, and bell pepper. Sauté until onion is limp. Stir in flour and cook for 1-2 minutes. Stir in broth. Bring to boiling and add potatoes. Cover and simmer until potatoes are tender (about 15 minutes). While waiting for the potatoes to cook, pour yourself a glass of wine. After sampling the wine, add the corn, chicken, and cream to the cooked potato mixture. Bring to a boil and season with salt and pepper to taste. Garnish with fresh, chopped cilantro and grated cheese at time of serving. Serves 4-6.

**Any cooked chicken will do, but poaching boneless, skinless chicken breasts in chicken broth with a little white wine is the best. Bring the chicken to a boil in liquid of choice. Let it simmer for 5-10 minutes and remove it from the heat. The meat juices should run clear when pierced with a fork. The breasts will be plump and tender. Allow them to cool before cutting into chunks. Add poaching liquid to the chowder.

Soups

* * * French Onion Soup

Onion soup is, among its other virtues, considered a delicious remedy for a hangover after an evening of partying. In Paris, small bistros stay open all night to serve wine and soup to late night and early morning party-goers.

Ingredients:

- 3 large white onions, thinly sliced or diced (diced is easier to eat)
- 3 tablespoons of butter
- 1 tablespoon of flour
- 1/2 teaspoon salt
- 1 teaspoon or more (I like lots of pepper) fresh cracked black pepper or more to taste
- 5 cups of beef broth
- 1 cup of red wine
- 4 thick slices of French or Italian bread
- 4 tablespoons or more of grated Parmesan cheese
- 4 tablespoons or more of grated Swiss or Gruyere cheese

Directions:

Melt butter in large heavy pan. Add the onions and cook slowly stirring occasionally until golden. It is important to cook until golden for the flavor changes. Sprinkle on the flour. Season with salt and pepper. After the onions are golden and the flour has cooked, add the wine and stir to deglaze the pan. Stir until wine has evaporated. Add beef broth and bring to a boil. Simmer partially covered for 30 minutes. (I like to make my soup a day ahead. The flavor is richer the next day.) Place a slice of French bread in each of 4 oven-proof bowls. Toast them first if you like. Preheat oven to broil. Sprinkle the bread with Parmesan cheese. Pour the soup over the bread and top with the Swiss or Gruyere cheese. Put bowls on metal tray and place under broiler. Cook until the cheese browns and serve immediately. Serves 4.

TIP:

One theory to keep from crying when peeling onions, is to put a cube of bread on the end of your knife, or to hold a piece of bread between your teeth. Bread absorbs fumes.

Soups

* * * MORSEL'S MARTINI MUSHROOM SOUP

Easy and delicious, this soup makes an astounding first course. White mushrooms and brown crimini have a mild earthy taste and are excellent in this soup. If you want to really excite the palate, try some wild mushrooms. The morel, shiitake, chanterelle, and enoki would add depth of flavor if mixed in with the cultivated mushrooms. If you use shiitake, do not use the stems.

Ingredients:

4-5 cups mushrooms, sliced
1/4 cup butter
2 cloves garlic, minced
1/4 cup flour
2 cups chicken broth
2 cups milk (Use whole milk for richness.)
1/2 cup fresh parsley, snipped
1/2 teaspoon salt
A few grinds of fresh nutmeg, or about 1/8 teaspoon of ground
Freshly ground black pepper to taste, 1/2 teaspoon or so
1/4 cup dry vermouth (To quality check the vermouth, have someone build you a martini. The vermouth could be optional. You could leave it out, but why would you?)

Directions:

After checking the quality of the vermouth, melt the butter in a very large saucepan or Dutch oven. Add the mushrooms and garlic. Cook and stir for about 5 minutes. Stir in the flour, blending well. Slowly add the broth and then the milk. Bring to a boil, stirring constantly. Reduce the heat and simmer for about 5 minutes. Add the parsley, salt, nutmeg, pepper, and vermouth. Continue cooking until heated through. Serves 8.

Note: This is a fun soup for parties because it is so easy to do. You just need a bigger pot for more mushrooms. (And a second martini!)

* * * * DON'T LIGHT A MATCH CHILI

Everyone has a favorite chili recipe. The list of ingredients is a mile long. But you just dump everything into a big soup kettle and forget it for about 2 hours. That's not so tough. Chili originated in Texas and is commonly referred to as a "bowl of red." (Texans don't add beans.) If you are experimenting with different kinds of chilies, a general rule of thumb is the larger the chili the milder the taste.

Ingredients:
2 12-ounce cans of beer
5 1/2 tablespoons chili powder
2 tablespoons ground cumin
1 tablespoon paprika
2 teaspoons beef bouillon granules
1 1/2 teaspoons dried oregano, or 3 teaspoons fresh
2-3 tablespoons olive oil
1 pound boneless beef chuck cut into 1/2-1 inch cubes
1 pound pork loin, cut into 1/2-1 inch cubes
1/2 teaspoon salt
1 teaspoon freshly ground black pepper
2 medium sized onions, chopped
1 Anaheim chili pepper, seeded and chopped
1 jalapeno pepper, seeded and chopped
5 cloves of garlic, minced
2 15-ounce cans tomato sauce
1 6-ounce can tomato paste
1 1/2 cups water
1 15 1/2-ounce can Mexican-style chili beans
1 16-ounce can red kidney beans
1/2 cup salsa
1 tablespoon ground coriander
2 teaspoons sugar
1 tablespoon fresh lime juice
Shredded cheddar cheese
Sour cream
Sliced ripe olives
Tortilla chips

Directions:
Brown meats in oil in a large skillet. Salt and pepper to taste. Transfer meat to a large soup kettle. Drink 1/2 can of beer and pour the rest into the kettle. Add chili powder, cumin, paprika, bouillon granules, and oregano. Bring mixture to a boil and remove from heat. In skillet sauté onions, garlic, and peppers over low heat until tender. Add more oil if needed. Transfer to the soup kettle. Stir in tomato sauce, coriander, salsa, sugar, tomato paste, water, and beans. Bring mixture to a boil, reduce heat and simmer covered for 2 hours. Just before serving, stir in lime juice. Serve chili with shredded cheddar cheese, sour cream, sliced olives, and tortilla chips.
Serves 10-12.

VEGETABLES

* * * MUSHROOMS IN CREAM SAUCE

I like to serve these with Cornish game hens instead of rice or potatoes. Use white mushrooms or the brown crimini. I think the crimini have a richer taste.

Ingredients:
1 1/2 pounds mushrooms
2 tablespoons unsalted butter
2 shallots (finely chopped) or 4 green onions, sliced
1/2 cup heavy cream
1-2 teaspoons salt (to taste)
1/4-1/2 teaspoon black pepper (I just take the pepper mill and crank away.)
1 teaspoon cornstarch dissolved in 1 tablespoon water
2 teaspoons cognac or brandy
1 tablespoon minced fresh chives

Directions:
Rinse mushrooms and drain. Cut larger ones in half. Sauté onions in melted butter about a minute. Add the mushrooms and sauté until tender, 6-8 minutes. If you don't have at least a cup of mushroom liquid in the pan, add some water. Add everything else except the chives. Cook to reduce and thicken sauce. Stir frequently. This step could take 15 minutes of so. Stir in the chives. Serve with thick slices of toasted bread or with poultry. Serves 6.

* * BACON BAKERS

This is a dynamic twist on the traditional baked potato. Thick slices of sweet onion are wedged between potato halves and the whole thing is wrapped in bacon. This could be a breakfast or an evening meal item.

Ingredients:
2 onions, thickly sliced
4 medium potatoes, sliced in half lengthwise. I prefer Yukon Gold.
8 strips of peppered bacon
Freshly ground black pepper

Directions:
Sprinkle potato halves lightly with black pepper. Layer onion on bottom half of potato. Top with other half of potato. Wrap bacon around potato and secure with toothpicks. Placed on lightly greased baking pan. Bake uncovered at 325 degrees for 1 1/2 hours or until potato is tender and bacon is crispy. Discard toothpicks. Serves 4.

Vegetables

* * * POTATOES WITH CREAM AND CHEESE

This basic gratin dish is absolutely delectable. Be sure to use Yukon Gold potatoes if you can, heavy cream, and freshly ground nutmeg.

Ingredients:
2 1/2 cups heavy cream
2 tablespoons butter
1 clove garlic, crushed
Freshly grated nutmeg, 2 to 3 grinds
6 Yukon Gold potatoes, thinly sliced (You do not have to peel the Yukons. If using russets, they should be peeled.)
1/2 cup Swiss cheese, grated
1/4 cup Parmesan cheese, grated
1/2 teaspoon salt
Freshly ground black pepper

Directions:
Place cream, butter, garlic, and nutmeg in a small saucepan. Simmer over low heat for 10 minutes, or until cream is reduced to about 2 cups and has thickened slightly. Butter a small casserole and layer 1/3 of the potatoes on the bottom of the dish. Add one third of the combined cheeses, season with salt and pepper and repeat to form 3 layers. Dot with butter. Add cream. There should be enough cream to cover the potatoes. Cover casserole and cook in a 300 degree oven for 1 hour or until potatoes are tender. Yield: 6 servings.

* * SKILLET POTATOES

These crusty and golden taters are great. Bake and serve them in a cast iron skillet for rustic effect.

Ingredients:
1/2 cup butter, melted
5 or 6 large potatoes, sliced (Yukons are best.)
2 sweet onions, thinly sliced and separated into rings
Salt and freshly ground black pepper to taste

Directions:
Brush a 10-inch cast iron skillet or a shallow baking dish with part of the melted butter. First, place a layer of potato slices in the pan with slices overlapping, then a layer of onion rings. Sprinkle with salt and pepper. Repeat layering, salting and peppering until all potatoes and onions are used up. Pour remaining melted butter over the potatoes. Bake uncovered at 450 degrees for 45 minutes or until the top is crusty and the potatoes are tender when pierced with a fork. Yield: 6 servings.

Vegetables

* * FIESTA HOMINY

Hominy is dried white or yellow corn kernels from which the hull and germ have been removed. This colorful dish has a zesty flavor. Tomatoes, bacon, green chilies, and peppers team up for a sideboard favorite. This is a great party recipe, because you can put it on early in the day and forget it.

Ingredients:

4 15 1/2-ounces cans hominy, drained (Use white or yellow or a combination
   of the two.)
1 14 1/2-ounce can diced tomatoes, undrained
1 10-ounce can diced tomatoes with green chilies, undrained
1 cup ketchup
1 cup medium salsa
1 8-ounce can tomato sauce
1 pound sliced bacon, cooked crisp and crumbled
1 large onion, chopped
1 medium green pepper, chopped

Directions:

In a slow cooker, combine the hominy, tomatoes, tomato sauce, ketchup, and salsa. In a skillet, cook bacon until crisp; drain on paper towels. Reserve 1 tablespoon of the drippings. Sauté onion and green pepper in drippings until tender. Stir onion mixture and bacon into hominy mixture. Cover and cook on low for 6-8 hours or until heated through. Serves 12.

* * * COMPANY GREEN BEANS

Water chestnuts and sour cream decidedly dress up green beans with flair. I like to use fresh beans and mushrooms in this recipe; however, frozen green beans and canned mushrooms will work okay.

Ingredients:
6 cups of whole green beans, cooked or 2 pounds frozen
2 cups fresh mushrooms, sliced or 2 4-ounce cans
2 tablespoons butter
1 8-ounce can sliced water chestnuts, drained
1 8-ounce carton sour cream
2 tablespoons onion, chopped
2 tablespoons flour
1 tablespoon butter, melted
1/2 teaspoon salt
Freshly ground black pepper
6 ounces Swiss cheese slices, torn into pieces

Directions:
Butter a 2 quart casserole. Cook beans and drain. Sauté mushrooms lightly in 2 tablespoons butter. In a large bowl, combine beans, mushrooms, water chestnuts, sour cream, onion, flour, butter, salt, and pepper. Gently stir in Swiss cheese. Spoon into prepared casserole. Bake covered at 400 degrees for 30 minutes or until heated through. Stir halfway through cooking. Serves 10.

* * * Pretty Peas

These little green sweet round balls that burst when you bite them are English peas. (The common garden pea.) It is definitely not so common in this recipe. The leeks, bacon, and sweet red pepper turn common into royalty.

Ingredients:
2 medium leeks
4 slices bacon, cooked crisp and crumbled
1 large sweet red bell pepper, julienned
2 10-ounce packages of frozen peas, thawed
1/2 cup chopped parsley
Salt and freshly ground black pepper

Directions:
Wash your leeks and cut them crosswise into thin slices. Sauté bacon until crisp and drain on paper towels. Reserve drippings. Add leeks and red pepper to pan and sauté in small amount of bacon drippings until tender. Stir in peas and half of the parsley, salt and pepper to taste, and heat through. Transfer to serving dish, sprinkle with bacon and remaining parsley. Serves 8.

Vegetables

* * * SHOWY CARROTS AND ZUCCHINI

Sweet carrots and tender small zucchinis are gently simmered with garlic and fresh thyme to create a showy side dish that is easy to prepare. There will be no more hiding the veggies under the plate when you serve this!

Ingredients:

2 large carrots, cut into 2 inch long and about 1/4 inch thick matchsticks
4 small zucchinis sliced into rounds
1 garlic clove cut in half
1 tablespoon olive oil
1 small onion, minced
1 teaspoon salt
1/4 teaspoon freshly ground pepper
1 teaspoon thyme
1/2 cup green onion, sliced
2 tablespoons water
2 tablespoons freshly grated Parmesan cheese
Fresh parsley, chopped for garnish

Directions:

Sauté the garlic in oil; remove from pan. Put onion in the same pan and cook slowly for about 10 minutes. Add the carrots, zucchinis, and green onions. Season with salt, pepper, and thyme. Add water. Cover and simmer gently for 15-20 minutes or until vegetables are tender. Drain; sprinkle with cheese and let stand covered for 5 minutes. Serve sprinkled with chopped parsley. Serves 6.

Vegetables

* * * SENSATIONAL SUMMER SQUASH

I have always loved anything that has been filled, stuffed, or sauced. So here is another "stuffed" type recipe. The yellow crookneck squash is such a cute little thing and prepared in this way will add uniqueness to a meal, not to mention great taste.

Ingredients:

5 small crookneck squash
1 teaspoon salt (about)
1/2 teaspoon freshly ground black pepper (or more)
1/2 cup chopped onion
1 clove garlic, minced
6 tablespoons butter
1 teaspoon Worcestershire sauce
1/8 teaspoon cayenne pepper
3 cups soft bread crumbs
1/4 cup freshly grated Parmesan
2 tablespoons diced pimento
Freshly grated Parmesan cheese, extra for garnish

Directions:

Wash squash and steam covered in salted water until tender. This should take about 30 minutes. Remove from water and cool. Cut off the ends and cut in half lengthwise. Scoop out the seeds. Season the squash with about 1/2 teaspoon salt and pepper and arrange in a baking pan that has been coated with cooking spray. Sauté the onion and garlic in butter until the onion is tender but not brown. Add the Worcestershire sauce, 1/2 teaspoon salt and the cayenne; toss with the bread crumbs, Parmesan cheese, and the diced pimento. Fill the squash shells with this mixture and bake in a hot oven 425 degrees for 20 minutes or until crumbs are brown. Sprinkle with freshly grated Parmesan cheese. Serves 10.

Vegetables

* * * SAUSAGE FILLED BAKED ONIONS

Most any onion will bake up nicely, but the summer sweetness of the Walla Walla Sweet onion really makes a difference in this dish. This is my Dad's favorite veggie dish and a great barbecue menu addition.

Ingredients:

6 medium to large onions
2 tablespoons olive oil
2 tablespoons green bell pepper, chopped
2 tablespoons sweet red bell pepper, chopped
3/4 pound Italian sausage
1 clove of garlic, minced
2 tablespoons ketchup
1/2 teaspoon salt
1/2 teaspoon freshly ground black pepper
1/4 cup dry Italian bread crumbs
1 cup chicken broth or water
1–2 tablespoons fresh parsley, chopped

Directions:

Peel the onions, cut off tops and scoop out centers. Do not cut into the base. Cook in boiling salted water until almost tender but firm enough to hold their shapes. Chop the centers of the onions and sauté in oil over medium heat with green and red peppers, sausage, and garlic. Break up the sausage as it cooks so that it is crumbly. It will be easier to work with when stuffing the onions. Add ketchup, salt, pepper, and bread crumbs. Mix and fill the onions with this mixture. Coat a baking dish with cooking spray. Place onions in prepared dish. Add a little water or chicken broth, cover and bake at 350 degrees for about 40 minutes. Baste onions occasionally as they bake. Sprinkle with parsley. Serves 6.

Vegetables

* * FRESH HERB SCALLOPED TOMATOES

Rendolent with fresh herbs and so easy to put together. This is a favorite. The use of canned tomatoes and packaged stuffing mix makes this not only easy but also fast. When fresh tomatoes are in season, I use those. It's really good either way.

Ingredients:

4 cups canned tomatoes, if using fresh; they need to be peeled.
2 1/3 cups packaged herb flavor stuffing mix
1 small onion, finely chopped
2 tablespoons sugar
1 tablespoon salt
1/2 teaspoon nutmeg
1 teaspoon fresh oregano or 1/2 teaspoon dried
3-4 fresh basil leaves, minced or 2 teaspoons dried
1/2 teaspoon freshly ground pepper
1/2 teaspoon fresh rosemary snipped or 1/4 teaspoon dried that has been ground (I use more rosemary, but I'm really fond of this highly aromatic and piney tasting herb.)
1/4 cup butter

Directions:

In a large bowl, mix together the tomatoes and all of the packaged stuffing mix except for 1/3 cup to be used later. Add the onion, sugar, salt, nutmeg, oregano, pepper, basil, and rosemary. Transfer tomato mixture to a buttered 2 quart casserole dish. Top the casserole with the last 1/3 cup of the stuffing mix and dot with butter. Bake at 375 degrees for 45 minutes. Serves 6-8.

A LITTLE EXTRA ABOUT HERBS

1. Use fresh whenever you can. If using dried, use half the amount of fresh. Also, be sure to crush dried herbs to release flavor-fragrant oils before using.
2. Fresh herbs can also be frozen for future use. Crumble while frozen to use. Do not thaw.
3. Fresh cut herbs have a so much more vivid and intense flavor than fresh packaged herbs at the supermarket. Have some of your own at home to snip.
4. Don't stop at using just the leaves. Many herbs have delicious tasting flowers (sage, basil, chives) and seeds (dill, fennel). These add beautiful color and flavor to salads, pasta, seafood, and bread.

Vegetables

* * * * KINDA QUICHE

Colorful fresh vegetables and fragrant, flavorful herbs abound in this quiche-like casserole dish. This is assembled the day before, so it's just one less thing to do on a busy day. Although I consider this an entrée, it could also be served as an hors d'oeuvre.

Ingredients:

1 loaf of Italian bread, about a pound, cut into 1/2 inch cubes.
1 can 14 1/2-ounce diced tomatoes, undrained
1 package 10-ounce frozen spinach, thawed and well drained
1 cup fresh mushrooms, sliced
2 cups shredded mozzarella cheese
1/2 cup sweet red bell pepper, chopped
1/2 cup green bell pepper, chopped
1 cup onion, chopped
2 green onions, sliced
3-4 fresh basil leaves torn, or 1 teaspoon dried
2 tablespoons fresh parsley, snipped
1 teaspoon fresh oregano leaves or about 1/2 teaspoon dried
1 cup milk
4 eggs beaten
1 teaspoon salt
Freshly ground black pepper

Directions:

Combine the first 12 ingredients in a large bowl and mix well. Transfer to a buttered 9x13x2 inch casserole dish. In a small bowl combine milk, eggs, salt, and pepper and pour over the vegetable mixture. Cover and refrigerate overnight. Remove from refrigerator 30 minutes before baking. Cover and bake at 425 degrees for 15 minutes. Uncover; bake 15 minutes longer or until a knife inserted near the center comes out clean. Serves 10.

Vegetables

INDEX BY RECIPE TITLE

A

A Little Extra About Herbs, 122
APPETIZERS:
  Biscuit Bundles, 3
  Cajun Power Wings, 5
  Celery with Gorgonzola, 7
  Chili Pastry Ole, 6
  Date-Garlic Bacon Bites, 4
  Divine Dill Dip, 7
  Mushroom Spread, 4
  Pastrami Bites, 3
  Pecans--Orange and Spicy, 5
  Sausage and Bacon Roll-ups, 6
Apple Puff, 26
Asparagus Pie, 23

B

Bacon Bakers, 115
Bacon Breakfast Burritos, 25
Baked Devil's Pasta, 61
Baked French Toast, 31
Baked Macaroni with Cheese, 66
Béarnaise Sauce, 28
Beefinsauzinbun, 52
Biscuit Bundles, 3
Black Pepper and Onion Bread, 11
Blueberry Preserves Coffee Cake, 44
Brandied Apricot and Raisin
  Cookies, 39
Bratzenbeefenlofe, 51
BREADS:
  Black Pepper and Onion Bread, 11
  Cherry Chocolate Bread, 11
  Dinner Rolls with Onion and
    Bacon, 15
  Fruit and Honey Bread, 13
  German Rye Bread, 12
  Ginger Scones, 19
  Granola Quick Bread, 17
  New York Apple Muffins, 14
  Rosemary and Black Olive Scones, 16
  Sausage Herb Muffins, 18

C

Cajun Power Wings, 5
Celery with Gorgonzola, 7
Cherry and Apple Coffee Cake, 45
Cherry Chocolate Bread, 11
Chicken BLT Salad, 88
Chicken Jalapeno Corn Chowder, 109
Chicken Salad Bundle, 96
Chicken Sandwich Extravaganza, 92
Chili Pastry Ole, 6
Chili Stuffed Chicken Breast, 73
Chocolate Chunk Biscotti, 37
Chocolate Nut and Spice Cake, 35
Chocolate-Peanut Butter Cake
  Squares, 46
Chocolate--Sweet, Seductive, and
  Smooth, 32
Christmas Lobster, 101
Clams in Thai Broth, 100
Coconut Cream Pie, 40
Company Green Beans, 118
Cornish Game Hens with Wine
  and Tarragon Sauce, 70
Creamy Baked Eggs, 24
Creamy Vegetable Chowder or
  Easter Soup, 107
Cucumber Sauce, 104
Curried Rice, 80

D

Date-Garlic Bacon Bites, 4
DESSERTS:
  Baked Strawberry Dessert, 36
  Blueberry Preserves Coffee Cake, 44
  Brandied Apricot and Raisin
    Cookies, 39
  Cherry and Apple Coffee Cake, 45
  Chocolate Chunk Biscotti, 37
  Chocolate Nut and Spice Cake, 35
  Chocolate-Peanut Butter Cake
    Squares, 46
  Coconut Cream Pie, 40

Index

Fresh Peach Cobbler, 42
Lemon Chiffon, 43
Petits Gateax, 38
Raspberry Cream Pie with Pecan Topping, 41
Dinner Rolls with Onion and Bacon, 15
Divine Dill Dip, 7
Don't Light A Match Chili, 112

E

Eggs--How To Poach Eggs, 27
Eggs--Martha's Cooking Tips for Eggs, 27

F

Farfalle with Mushroom Sauce, 65
Fennel and Red Onion Salad, 85
Festive Frittata, 29
Fettuccine Tossed with Crab and Asparagus, 64
Fiesta Hominy, 117
French Onion Soup, 110
Fresh Herbed Scalloped Tomatoes, 122
Fresh Peach Cobbler, 42
Fruit and Honey Bread, 13

G

German Rye Bread, 12
Ginger Scones, 19
Glazed and Stuffed Pork Loin Roast, 56
Golden Turkey Bake, 69
Granola Quick Bread, 17

H

Ham and Broccoli Brunch Pastry, 30
Ham and Cheddar Pasta Toss, 87
Hearts of Palm and Asparagus Salad, 86
Herbed Rib Eye Steaks, 49
Hide the Salami, 94
Honey Grilled Chicken with Sweet Cherries, 74

How to Poach Eggs, 27

I

Italian Sausage Meatball Stew, 108

K

Kinda Quiche, 123

L

Lemon Chiffon, 43
Linguine and Shrimp with Gingered Sauce, 63

M

Martha Burger (The), 91
Martha's Cooking Tips for Eggs, 20
MEATS:
   Beefinsauzinbun, 52
   Bratzenbeefenlofe, 51
   Glazed and Stuffed Pork Loin Roast, 56
   Herbed Rib Eye Steaks, 49
   Peppered Flank Steak, 55
   Pork Ribs Polynesian, 58
   Pork Tenderloin Stir Fry, 57
   Rack of Lamb with Herb Crust, 53
   Rouladen, 50
   Terrific Tournedos, 54
Morsel's Martini Mushroom Soup, 111
Mushroom and Bacon Benedict, 27
Mushroom Spread, 4
Mushrooms in Cream Sauce, 115

N

New York Apple Muffins, 14

O

Orange and Pear Salad, 84

P

PASTA:

Index

Baked Devil's Pasta, 61
Baked Macaroni with Cheese, 66
Farfalle with Mushroom Sauce, 65
Fettuccine Tossed with Crab and
   Asparagus, 64
Ham and Cheddar Pasta Toss, 87
Linguine with Shrimp and Gingered
   Sauce, 63
Spaghetti with Bacon, 62
Pastrami Bites, 3
Pecans--Orange and Spicy, 5
Peppered Flank Steak, 55
Petits Gateax, 38
Pizza Puff, 93
Pork Ribs Polynesian, 58
Pork Tenderloin Stir Fry, 57
Potatoes with Cream and Cheese, 116
POULTRY:
   Chili Stuffed Chicken Breast, 73
   Cornish Game Hens with Wine and
      Tarragon Sauce, 70
   Golden Turkey Bake, 69
   Honey Grilled Chicken with
      Sweet Cherries, 74
   Roast Duckling with Orange
      Sauce, 72
   Tarragon Chicken in Champagne
      Sauce, 71

R

Rack of Lamb with Herb Crust, 53
Raspberry Cream Pie with Pecan
   Topping, 41
Raspberry Salad, 85
RICE:
   Curried Rice, 80
   Herbed Rice with Tomatoes and
      Basil, 77
   Rice with Green Peppers and
      Onions, 78
   Rice with Tomatoes and Bacon, 79
   Water Chestnuts and Rice, 77
   Wild Rice with Sausage, 79
   Wild Rice with Sautéed Almonds, 78
Roast Duckling with Orange Sauce, 72
Roasted Garlic Paste, 54
Rosemary and Black Olive Scones, 16

Rouladen, 50

S

SALADS:
   Chicken BLT Salad, 88
   Fennel and Red Onion Salad, 85
   Ham and Cheddar Pasta Toss, 87
   Hearts of Palm and Asparagus
      Salad, 86
   Orange and Pear Salad, 84
   Raspberry Salad, 85
   Special Salad, 83
Salmon in Lemon Cream, 104
SANDWICHES:
   Beefinsauzinbun, 52
   Chicken Salad Bundle, 96
   Chicken Sandwich Extravaganza, 92
   Hide the Salami, 94
   Martha Burger (The), 91
   Pizza Puff, 93
   Spicy Steak and Onion Sandwich, 95
Sausage and Bacon Roll-ups, 6
Sausage Herb Muffins, 18
Scalloped Oysters, 103
Scallops in Creamy Ginger Sauce, 102
SEAFOOD:
   Clams in Thai Broth, 100
   Christmas Lobster, 101
   Salmon in Lemon Cream, 104
   Scalloped Oysters, 103
   Scallops in Creamy Ginger Sauce, 102
   Swordfish with Salsa, 99
Sensational Summer Squash, 120
Showy Carrots and Zucchini, 119
Skillet Potatoes, 116
SOUPS:
   Chicken Jalapeno Corn Chowder, 109
   Creamy Vegetable Chowder or
      Easter Soup, 107
   Don't Light A Match Chili, 112
   French Onion Soup, 110
   Italian Sausage Meatball Stew, 108
   Morsel's Martini Mushroom Soup,
      111
Spaghetti with Bacon, 62
Special Ideas for Special Times, 8
Special Salad, 83

Index

Spicy Steak and Onion Sandwich, 95
Swordfish with Salsa, 99

T

Tarragon Chicken in Champagne Sauce, 71
Terrific Tournedos, 54

V

VEGETABLES:
  Bacon Bakers, 115
  Company Green Beans, 118
  Fiesta Hominy, 117
  Fresh Herb Scalloped Tomatoes, 122
  Kinda Quiche, 123
  Mushrooms in Cream Sauce, 115
  Potatoes with Cream and Cheese, 116
  Pretty Peas, 118
  Sausage Filled Baked Onions, 121
  Sensational Summer Squash, 120
  Showy Carrots and Zucchini, 119
  Skillet Potatoes, 116

W

Wild Rice with Sausage, 79
Wild Rice with Sautéed Almonds, 78
Water Chestnuts and Rice, 77

Z

Zesty Dill Sauce

INDEX BY MAIN INGREDIENT & TOPIC

A

APPETIZERS:
  Biscuit Bundles, 3
  Cajun Power Wings, 5
  Celery with Gorgonzola, 7
  Chili Pastry Ole, 6
  Date-Garlic Bacon Bites, 4
  Divine Dill Dip, 7
  Mushroom Spread, 4
  Pastrami Bites, 3
  Pecans--Orange and Spicy, 5
  Sausage and Bacon Roll-ups, 6
Apple Coffee Cake--Cherry and Apple Coffee Cake, 45
Apple Muffins--New York Apple Muffins, 14
Apple Puff, 26
Apricot--Brandied Apricot and Raisin Cookies, 39
Asparagus--Fettuccine Tossed with Crab and Asparagus, 64
Asparagus Pie, 23
Asparagus Salad--Hearts of Palm And Asparagus Salad, 86

B

BACON:
  Bacon Bakers, 115
  Bacon Breakfast Burritos, 25
  BLT Chicken Salad, 88
  Mushroom and Bacon Benedict, 27
  Rice with Tomatoes and Bacon, 79
  Sausage and Bacon Roll-ups, 6
  Spaghetti with Bacon, 62
Beans--Company Green Beans, 118
BEEF:
  Beefinsauzinbun, 52
  Bratzenbeefenlofe, 51
  Don't Light A Match Chili, 112
  Herbed Rib Eye Steaks, 49
  Peppered Flank Steak, 55
  Rouladen, 50
  • Spicy Steak and Onion Sandwiches, 95
  Terrific Tournedos, 54

Biscotti--Chocolate Chunk Biscotti, 37
Blueberry Preserves Coffee Cake, 44
Brandied Apricot and Raisin Cookies, 39
BREADS:
  Biscuit Bundles, 3
  Black Pepper and Onion Bread, 11
  Cherry Chocolate Bread, 11
  Dinner Rolls with Onion and Bacon, 15
  Fruit and Honey Bread, 13
  German Rye Bread, 12
  Ginger Scones, 19
  Granola Quick Bread, 17
  New York Apple Muffins, 14
  Rosemary and Black Olive Scones, 16
  Sausage Herb Muffins, 18
BREAKFAST or BRUNCH:
  Apple Puff, 26
  Asparagus Pie, 23
  Bacon Breakfast Burritos, 25
  Baked French Toast, 31
  Béarnaise Sauce, 28
  Creamy Baked Eggs, 24
  Festive Frittata, 29
  Ham and Broccoli Brunch Pastry, 30
  Mushroom and Bacon Benedict, 27

C

Cajun Power Wings, 5
CAKES:
  Blueberry Preserves Coffee Cake, 44
  Cherry and Apple Coffee Cake, 45
  Chocolate Nut and Spice Cake, 35
  Chocolate-Peanut Butter Cake Squares, 46
Carrots--Showy Carrots and Zucchini, 119
Celery with Gorgonzola, 7
Champagne Sauce--Tarragon Chicken in Champagne Sauce, 71
Cheese--Baked Macaroni with Cheese, 66
Cheese--Potatoes with Cream and Cheese, 116
Cherries--Sweet Cherries with Honey Grilled Chicken, 74

Cherry and Apple Coffee Cake, 45
Cherry Chocolate Bread, 11
CHICKEN:
  BLT--Chicken BLT Salad, 88
  Cajun Power Wings, 5
  Chicken Jalapeno Corn Chowder, 109
  Chicken Salad Bundle, 96
  Chicken Sandwich Extravaganza, 92
  Chili Stuffed Chicken Breasts, 73
  Honey Grilled Chicken with Sweet Cherries, 74
  Tarragon Chicken in Champagne Sauce, 71
Chili--Don't Light A Match Chili, 112
Chili Pastry Ole, 6
CHOCOLATE:
  Cherry Chocolate Bread, 11
  Chocolate Chunk Biscotti, 37
  Chocolate Nut and Spice Cake, 35
  Chocolate-Peanut Butter Cake Squares, 46
  Chocolate--Sweet, Seductive, and Smooth, 32
Clams in Thai Broth, 100
Cobbler--Fresh Peach Cobbler, 42
Coconut Cream Pie, 40
COOKIES:
  Brandied Apricot and Raisin Cookies, 39
  Chocolate Chunk Biscotti, 37
  Petits Gateax, 38
Corn Chowder--Chicken Jalapeno Corn Chowder, 109
Cornish Game Hens with Wine and Tarragon Sauce, 70
Crab--Fettuccine Tossed with Crab and Asparagus, 64
Cream Sauce--Mushrooms in Cream Sauce, 115
Creamy Baked Eggs, 24
Creamy Vegetable Chowder or Easter Soup, 107
Cucumber Sauce, 104
Curried Rice, 80

D

Date-Garlic Bacon Bites, 4
DESSERTS:
  Baked Strawberry Dessert, 36
  Blueberry Preserves Coffee Cake, 44
  Brandied Apricot and Raisin Cookies, 39
  Cherry and Apple Coffee Cake, 45
  Chocolate Chunk Biscotti, 37
  Chocolate Nut and Spice Cake, 35
  Chocolate-Peanut Butter Cake Squares, 46
  Coconut Cream Pie, 40
  Fresh Peach Cobbler, 42
  Lemon Chiffon, 43
  Petits Gateax, 38
  Raspberry Cream Pie with Pecan Topping, 41
Dill Dip--Divine Dill Dip, 7
Dill Sauce--Zesty Dill Sauce, 103

E

EGGIE STUFF:
  Asparagus Pie, 23
  Bacon Breakfast Burritos, 25
  Creamy Baked Eggs, 24
  Eggs--How to Poach Eggs, 27
  Eggs--Martha's Cooking Tips for Eggs, 20
  Festive Frittata, 29
  Kinda Quiche, 123
  Mushroom and Bacon Benedict, 27

F

Farfalle with Mushroom Sauce, 65
Fennel and Red Onion Salad, 85
Festive Frittata, 29
Fettuccine Tossed with Crab and Asparagus, 64
Fiesta Hominy, 117
Flank Steak--Peppered Flank Steak 55
French Onion Soup, 110
French Toast--Baked, 31
Fruit and Honey Bread, 13

G

Game Hens--Cornish Game Hens with Wine and Tarragon Sauce, 70
Garlic-Date, Garlic Bacon Bites, 4
Garlic Paste--Roasted Garlic Paste, 53

Index

Ginger Sauce--Scallops in Creamy Ginger Sauce, 102
Ginger Scones, 19
Gingered Sauce--Linguini and Shrimp with Gingered Sauce, 63
Gorgonzola--Celery with Gorgonzola, 7
Green Beans--Company Green Beans, 118
Green Peppers--Rice with Onions and Green Peppers, 78

H

Ham and Broccoli Brunch Pastry, 30
Ham and Cheddar Pasta Toss, 87
Hearts of Palm and Asparagus Salad, 86
Herb Crust--Rack of Lamb in Herb Crust, 53
Herb Muffins--Sausage Herb Muffins, 18
Herb Tomatoes--Fresh Herb Scalloped Tomatoes 122
Herbed Rib Eye Steaks, 49
Herbed Rice with Tomatoes and Basil, 77
Herbs--A Little About Herbs, 122
Hominy--Fiesta Hominy, 117
Honey Grilled Chicken with Sweet Cherries, 74

J

Jalapeno--Chicken Jalapeno Corn Chowder, 109

L

Lamb--Rack of Lamb with Herb Crust, 53
Linguine and Shrimp with Gingered Sauce, 63
Lobster--Christmas Lobster, 101

M

Macaroni--Baked Macaroni with Cheese, 66
Meatball Stew--Italian Sausage Meatball Stew, 108

Muffins--New York Apple Muffins, 14
Muffins--Sausage Herb Muffins, 18
MUSHROOMS:
  Farfalle with Mushroom Sauce, 65
  Morsel's Martini Mushroom Soup, 111
  Mushroom and Bacon Benedict, 27
  Mushroom Spread, 4
  Mushrooms in Cream Sauce, 115

O

ONION:
  Dinner Rolls with Onion and Bacon, 15
  Fennel and Red Onion Salad, 85
  French Onion Soup, 110
  Rice with Green Peppers and Onions, 78
  Sausage Filled Baked Onions, 121
  Spicy Steak and Onion Sandwiches, 95
Orange and Pear Salad, 84
Orange Sauce--Roast Duckling with Orange Sauce, 72
Oysters--Scalloped, 103

P

PASTA:
  Baked Devil's Pasta, 61
  Baked Macaroni with Cheese, 66
  Farfalle with Mushroom Sauce, 65
  Fettuccine Tossed with Crab and Asparagus, 64
  Ham and Cheddar Pasta Toss, 87
  Linguine and Shrimp with Gingered Sauce, 63
  Spaghetti with Bacon, 62
Pastrami Bites, 3
Peach Cobbler--Fresh Peach Cobbler, 42
Pear Salad--Orange and Pear Salad, 84
Peas--Pretty Peas, 118
Pecans--Orange and Spicy, 5
Pepper--Black Pepper Onion Bread, 11
Peppered Flank Steak, 55
PIE:
  Asparagus Pie, 23
  Coconut Cream Pie, 40

Index

Raspberry Cream Pie with Pecan
    Filling, 41
Pizza Puff, 93
PORK:
  Pork Loin--Glazed and Stuffed Pork
    Loin Roast, 56
  Pork Ribs Polynesian, 58
  Pork Tenderloin Stir Fry, 57
Potatoes--Skillet Potatoes, 116
Potatoes with Cream and Cheese, 116
POULTRY:
  Cajun Power Wings, 5
  Chicken BLT Salad, 88
  Chili Stuffed Chicken Breasts, 73
  Cornish Game Hens with Wine and
    Tarragon Sauce, 70
  Golden Turkey Bake, 69
  Honey Grilled Chicken with
    Sweet Cherries, 74
  Roast Duckling with Orange Sauce,
    72
  Tarragon Chicken in Champagne
    Sauce, 71

Q

Quiche--Kinda Quiche, 123
Quick Bread--Granola Quick Bread, 17

R

Rack of Lamb, 53
Raisin--Brandied Apricot and Raisin
  Cookies, 39
Raspberry Cream Pie with Pecan
  Topping, 41
Raspberry Salad, 85
Rib Eye--Herbed Rib Eye Steak, 49
Ribs--Polynesian Pork Ribs, 58
RICE:
  Curried Rice, 80
  Herbed Rice with Tomatoes and
    Basil, 77
  Rice with Green Peppers and Onions,
    78
  Rice with Tomatoes and Bacon, 79
  Water Chestnuts and Rice, 77
  Wild Rice with Sausage, 79
  Wild Rice with Sautéed Almonds, 78
Roast Duckling with Orange Sauce, 72

Roast Pork--Glazed and Stuffed Pork
  Loin Roast, 56
Roasted Garlic Paste, 54
Rolls--Dinner Rolls with Onion and
  Bacon, 15
Rosemary and Black Olive Scones, 16
Rouladen, 50
Rye Bread--German Rye Bread, 12

S

SALADS:
  Chicken BLT Salad, 88
  Fennel and Red Onion Salad, 85
  Ham and Cheddar Pasta Toss, 87
  Hearts of Palm and Asparagus
    Salad, 86
  Orange and Pear Salad, 84
  Raspberry Salad, 85
  Special Salad, 83
Salami--Hide the Salami, 94
Salmon in Lemon Cream, 104
SANDWICHES:
  Beefinsauzinbun, 52
  Chicken Salad Bundle, 96
  Chicken Sandwich Extravaganza,
    92
  Hide the Salami, 94
  Martha Burger (The), 91
  Pizza Puff, 93
  Spicy Steak and Onion Sandwich, 95
SAUCES:
  Béarnaise Sauce, 28
  Champagne Sauce--Tarragon
    Chicken in Champagne Sauce, 71
  Cream Sauce--Mushrooms in Cream
    Sauce, 115
  Cucumber Sauce, 104
  Ginger Sauce--Creamy Scallops in
    Ginger Sauce, 102
  Mushroom Sauce--Farfalle with
    Mushroom Sauce, 65
  Orange Sauce--Roast Duckling with
    Orange Sauce, 72
  Tarragon Sauce--Cornish Game Hens
    in Wine and Tarragon Sauce, 70
  Zesty Dill Sauce, 103
SAUSAGE:
  Italian Sausage Meatball Stew, 108
  Sausage and Bacon Roll-ups, 6

Index

Sausage Filled Baked Onions, 121
  Sausage Herb Muffins, 18
  Wild Rice with Sausage, 79
Scalloped Oysters, 103
Scalloped Tomatoes--Fresh Herb Scalloped Tomatoes, 122
Scallops in Creamy Ginger Sauce, 102
Scones--Ginger Scones, 19
Scones--Rosemary and Black Olive Scones, 16
SEAFOOD:
  Christmas Lobster, 101
  Clams in Thai Broth, 100
  Salmon in Lemon Cream, 104
  Scalloped Oysters, 103
  Scallops in Creamy Ginger Sauce, 102
  Shrimp Linguini with Gingered Sauce, 63
  Swordfish with Salsa, 99
SOUPS:
  Chicken Jalapeno Corn Chowder, 109
  Creamy Vegetable Chowder or Easter Soup, 107
  Don't Light A Match Chili, 112
  Fiesta Hominy, 117
  French Onion Soup, 110
  Italian Sausage Meatball Stew, 108
  Morsel's Martini Mushroom Soup, 111
Spaghetti with Bacon, 62
Special Ideas for Special Times, 8
Special Salad, 83
Spicy--Pecans Orange and Spicy, 5
Spicy Steak and Onion Sandwiches, 95
Squash--Sensational Summer Squash, 120
Steak--Peppered Flank Steak, 55
Steak Sandwich--Spicy Steak and Onion Sandwich, 95
Steaks--Herbed Rib Eye Steaks, 49
Stir Fry--Pork Tenderloin Stir Fry, 57

T

Tarragon Chicken in Champagne Sauce, 71

Tarragon Sauce--Cornish Game Hens with Wine and Tarragon Sauce, 70
Tenderloin--Pork Tenderloin Stir Fry, 57
Terrific Tournedos, 54
Thai Broth--Clams in Thai Broth, 100
Toast--Baked French Toast, 31
TOMATOES:
  Fresh Herbed Scalloped Tomatoes, 122
  Herbed Rice with Basil and Tomatoes, 77
  Rice with Tomatoes and Bacon, 79
Turkey Bake--Golden Turkey Bake, 69

V

VEGETABLES:
  Bacon Bakers, 115
  Company Green Beans, 118
  Fiesta Hominy, 117
  Fresh Herb Scalloped Tomatoes, 122
  Kinda Quiche, 123
  Mushrooms in Cream Sauce, 115
  Potatoes with Cream and Cheese, 116
  Pretty Peas, 118
  Sausage Filled Baked Onions, 121
  Sensational Summer Squash, 120
  Showy Carrots and Zucchini, 119
  Skillet Potatoes, 116
Vegetable Chowder--Creamy Vegetable Chowder or Easter Soup, 107

W

Water Chestnuts and Rice, 77
Wild Rice with Sausage, 79
Wild Rice with Sautéed Almonds, 78
Wings--Cajun Power Wings, 5

Z

Zesty Dill Sauce, 103
Zucchini--Showy Carrots and Zucchini, 119

Index